LATIMER STUDIES 67

HERESY, SCHISM AND APOSTASY

BY GERALD BRAY

The Latimer Trust

© Gerald Bray 2008

ISBN 978-0-946307-61-6

Published by the Latimer Trust

PO Box 26685

London N14 4XQ

www.latimertrust.org

Contents

1. **Humpty Dumpty's church?** 1

1.1. The current crisis 1

1.2. Comprehensiveness and its limits 3

1.3. The weight of history 11

2. **Spiritual experience, theological orthodoxy and Anglicanism** 16

2.1. The fundamental importance of spiritual experience 16

2.2. Why spiritual experience is not enough 27

2.3. The emergence of orthodoxy 31

2.4. The church and its teachers 34

2.5. Catholic orthodoxy and Anglicanism 39

3. **Heresy** 45

3.1. The origin of the concept 45

3.2. Heresy as a capital crime 48

3.3. Heresy trials in modern times 51

3.4. The doctrinal paralysis of the modern church 56

3.5. Dealing with heresy today 59

4. **Schism** 66

4.1.   *Division in the church* 66

4.2.   *The current scene* 69

5. **Apostasy** 74

5.1.   *Abandoning the Christian faith altogether* 74

5.2.   *The current crisis* 77

6. **Orthodoxy and the future of Anglicanism** ...79

6.1.   *Orthodoxy and Anglicanism* 79

6.2.   *Form and substance* 83

6.3.   *Word and Spirit* 85

6.4.   *Biblical interpretation and hermeneutics* 87

6.5.   *Theological renewal* 94

6.6.   *The way ahead* 95

1. Humpty Dumpty's church?

1.1. The current crisis

As everyone knows, the Anglican Communion has recently been riven by divisions which have threatened its unity and integrity.[1] Words like 'heresy' and 'schism' have been bandied about by the different protagonists with little thought as to what they mean. We have even seen bishops travel half way round the world to minister to individuals and parishes who cannot accept the ministry of their local diocesans because they are convinced that the latter have departed from the 'faith once delivered to the saints', and in England more than one parish has refused to make financial contributions to its diocese for essentially the same reason. What justification do these dissidents have for their actions? Does their assessment of their own bishops have any objective foundation? If a bishop crosses diocesan boundaries to minister to such people, does he create a schism by his actions, or is he simply bearing witness to a division that already exists and is only waiting to be articulated in structural terms?

Those who take such actions assume that there is a norm of Christian belief to which everyone in the church is expected to subscribe, but what is that norm and who determines when it has been disregarded? Unlike some other Christian bodies, the Anglican Communion has never claimed to be the only true church, nor does it accept that any bishop, council or congregation can claim to be infallible.[2] It must therefore be possible for even its most hallowed traditions to be mistaken, at least to some degree, and Anglicans have never denied this, even if the church's practice has not always matched its theory. A good example of how theory

---

[1] Similar divisions have also appeared in Reformed, Lutheran and Methodist churches and elements of them are present almost everywhere, but the Anglican Communion stands out as the place where they have come to a head most sharply.

[2] See Articles 19-21.

and practice can get out of step and lead to some dubious consequences is the Anglican attitude towards the monarchical form of episcopacy. The Ordinal of 1550 states in its preface:

> It is evident unto all men diligently reading Holy Scripture and ancient authors, that from the Apostles' time there have been these orders of ministers in Christ's church – bishops, priests and deacons.

On the basis of that assertion, the Church of England has long refused to recognise clergymen who have not been episcopally ordained and the Anglican Communion still insists on the so-called 'monarchical' episcopate as an essential component of full communion with other churches.[3] However, it is now universally recognized (even by Roman Catholics) that historical research has shown that the Ordinal's statement is inaccurate and misleading, although it was made in good faith at the time. Neither in the New Testament nor in the immediate post-Apostolic literature is there any clear evidence that churches were governed by a single bishop, and it is probable that some form of collective leadership persisted into the second century, particularly at Rome. The Ordinal's claim about the threefold structure of holy orders cannot be made today without serious qualification, and Anglican practice now has to be justified on other grounds. It is true that the hierarchy of orders as we know it developed out of the Apostolic church over time and was not seriously contested for 1300 years, so it may be reasonable to retain it on that basis, but to say that it was of Apostolic institution is going too far. Most Anglicans realise this, but the church has not yet faced up to the consequences this realisation must have for ecumenical relations and continues to act as if the 'historic episcopate' is a necessary ingredient of a truly Apostolic

---

[3] The absurdity of this can be seen from the effects of the recent (1995) Porvoo Agreement between the Anglican churches of the British Isles and the Lutheran churches of Scandinavia and the Baltic States. The church of Denmark has refused to ratify the agreement because it rejects any notion of 'apostolic succession' in the historic episcopate, but it remains in full communion with the church of Norway, which has ratified it and is in full communion with the British Anglican churches. Meanwhile the latter remain out of communion with other Reformed churches in Europe, even though historically and theologically they have much more in common with them than they do with the Lutherans.

church.

But if something as fundamental to Anglican identity as its episcopate can be shown to lack the authority officially claimed for it, why should the same not be true of other things as well? For example, the doctrine of the Trinity is not explicitly set out in the New Testament and the Apostles never confessed the creeds which expound it, so why should it be a necessary part of Christian belief? Here we are treading on delicate ground, because although no-one can now reject the 'historic episcopate' and remain an Anglican, there have been both clergy and bishops who have denied the Trinity yet escaped church discipline. Does this mean that the episcopate is essential to Anglicanism while the Trinity is just a matter of theological opinion that can be discarded with impunity? This would seem to be a complete inversion of priorities, but the history of the church confirms that questions of order have often been more important than the fundamental tenets of the faith and they remain so when it comes to deciding who is in communion with us and who is not. Is this right, and if not, what (if anything) can be done about it?

1.2. Comprehensiveness and its limits

Anglicanism is often characterised as a 'comprehensive' church which includes a wide range of different views in its ranks. Some claim that its formularies and patterns of worship are so broadly constructed that they can legitimately be read in many different ways, and studied ambiguity often seems to be one of the chief features of its official statements. Apologists for this state of affairs like to glory in Anglicanism's apparent 'freedom', but to others it seems that we are like Humpty Dumpty, who claimed that words mean whatever their speakers want them to mean, and that no authority exists who can tell them they are wrong. As an Anglican, you can believe that the resurrection of Jesus was a historical fact or you can say that it was a spiritual experience expressed in pseudo-historical terms, without falling foul of the church's discipline. You can claim that the Bible is the eternal Word of God, meant to be obeyed by all Christians in every age and culture, or say that it is nothing more than an important collection of ancient literature which reflects the thoughts and prejudices of its many authors, and still remain within the bosom of the church. Incompatible beliefs about the ministry, the sacraments and almost anything one cares to name can and do co-exist under the Anglican umbrella, and nobody seems to be able to say what the boundaries of the church's faith are.

Opponents of this modern 'comprehensiveness' believe that the degree of latitude currently permitted within Anglicanism has been achieved by intellectual sleight of hand. They point out that the Thirty-nine Articles of Religion make it clear that Holy Scripture is the only recognised source of true doctrine and that one part of it must not be expounded in a way which contradicts another part.[4] In their view, the Bible contains a coherent body of Christian teaching which forms the substance of the church's doctrine. If the church is teaching something that cannot be found in the Bible either explicitly or by reasonable inference from the text, then that teaching must either be removed or made an optional extra not to be imposed on anyone as a matter of belief. This is what the Protestant Reformers of the sixteenth century were trying to do. For example, the medieval church had been teaching a doctrine of transubstantiation which is not in the Bible and cannot be inferred from it, so they dropped it.[5] They also rejected the medieval doctrine of purgatory for the same reasons.[6] But the doctrine of the Trinity was retained because although it is not stated as such in the Bible, it is the only way that the relationship of the Father, the Son and the Holy Spirit described in the New Testament can be properly understood. The Reformers knew that it had taken the church many centuries to figure this out in detail, but they recognised that the substance of Trinitarian teaching was there from the beginning and that the definitions arrived at in the fourth and fifth centuries had stood the test of time.[7]

The divine inspiration of the Bible was taken for granted in

---

[4] See Articles 5 and 20.
[5] Article 28.
[6] Article 22.
[7] It must be remembered that the doctrine was objected to in the sixteenth century and later by the followers of Lauro and Fausto Sozzini (Socinus). The Socinians are now called Unitarians.

the sixteenth century and so the Thirty-nine Articles assume it, just as they assume that their interpretation of the sacred text is self-evidently correct. This was less of a problem then than it seems to us now, because all the disputants in the Reformation had been trained in the principles of Erasmian humanism and were fundamentally agreed about what the Bible said and meant. The dispute with Rome was not about that, but about the extent to which tradition should be allowed to supplement the Bible and determine its use in the life of the church. The Roman argument was that Scripture by itself was not enough to decide questions of doctrine and that other factors had to be given due weight. The issue of papal primacy, for example, was based on the words of Jesus to Peter in Matthew 16:18: 'You are Peter, and on this rock I shall build my church', but when the Reformers objected that this verse did not justify the conclusions which the medieval church had come to, the Roman reply was that it had to be interpreted in the light of historical developments which had revealed its deeper meaning. This is still the basic difference between Protestant and Roman Catholic interpretations of verses like this one, as modern ecumenical discussions have made clear. It is not so much the text itself but the significance of the way it has been used over the centuries that constitutes the main point at issue. This explains why, in recent ecumenical dialogues, Catholic partners have generally tried to get Protestants to accept the validity of their traditional understanding, even when they agree with Protestants that it is not inherent in the biblical text itself.

The willingness of some modern Protestants to consider accepting Catholic tradition as valid does not come from any new discovery about the meaning of the Bible, but from an increasing lack of confidence in the viability of the doctrinal principle of *sola Scriptura* as this was understood by the Reformers. Today we are more conscious than they were of the 'humanness' of Scripture and recognise that the books of the Bible were composed in different circumstances, most of which are unclear to us. Their authors were circumscribed by limitations which are reflected in their work, and although we can reasonably claim that they were not trying to deceive people, that does not mean that they always got things 'right' or that we are compelled to take what they wrote as 'true' in an absolute sense that transcends any kind of historical relativity. It does not even exclude the possibility that one author of Scripture may contradict another, either because the circumstances being addressed were different or because they had other ideas about God and his ways with man. The Reformers had already met a classical example of this in the supposed incompatibility between Paul, who believed that a person is justified by faith without works of any kind, and James, who said that faith without works is dead.[8] They resolved this by saying that Paul was talking about the ground of justification whereas James was concerned with its fruits in the Christian life, a distinction which is supported by their respective contexts, though it is surprising how often this example is still cited today as evidence of a 'contradiction' in Scripture!

Modern scholarship has gone much further than this, of course, and turned up all kinds of apparent inconsistencies which the Reformers would not have recognised. The Pentateuch is now attributed to different sources which have been cobbled together but which continue to reflect a variety of origins, and the Gospels also retain the memory of the different oral traditions that went into their composition. Tensions in ancient Judaism can be detected in the prophets and competing schools of thought are held to underlie the Pauline and Johannine approaches to early Christianity, whose differences can be explained by the conflicts between them. In addition to this, there are now many competing hermeneutical approaches to Scripture, and for the church to tie a modern person's conscience to sixteenth-century interpretations of it seems absurd to many people today.

Some 'conservative' Anglicans are untroubled by these developments because they do not recognise the Reformers' insistence on the authority of Scripture alone as fundamental for the church's life and doctrine. In their view, Anglicanism is a branch of the Catholic Church on a par with Rome and the Eastern Churches, and only what it holds in common with those bodies can be regarded as truly authoritative. Since we now live in a divided Christendom, whatever distinctive doctrines Anglicans assert (and these would include many of the Thirty-nine Articles) are merely

---

[8] Compare Galatians 2:16 with James 2:26.

tentative – the products of a broken body of Christ, which will have to be adjusted if and when that body is ever put together again. In theory, these Catholic Anglicans also believe that doctrines accepted only by the Roman Catholic Church (like the infallibility of the pope or the perpetual virginity of Mary) will also be subject to revision at some point in the future, but in practice many of them accept whatever Rome has decreed, and regard the papacy as the final arbiter in matters of Christian doctrine.[9] From an Evangelical point of view, the trouble with this is that although these people are strong supporters of (pre-Reformation) orthodoxy, they do not believe in their own church's view of authority, and it is hard to understand why they remain Anglicans at all. In fact, over the years many have left and become Roman Catholics, as John Henry Newman did in 1845. This would seem to be the logical outcome of their beliefs and although we must be sorry to see anyone leave the Anglican Communion, it is surely better for them to go than to undermine it from within in the name of 'catholicism'. Anglicans certainly ought to have a high regard for the universal church and respect everyone who holds the fundamental doctrines of the Christian faith, whatever disagreements may exist on many other matters, but if people deny the validity of their own church's beliefs the only honest thing for them to do is to leave it.

At the other end of the spectrum are people who believe that if we are to remain faithful to our inheritance we must update it and bring it into line with wider changes in society. In the view of these people, the early church succeeded because it spoke to the spirit of the times, but times have now changed. If we continue to use the ancient Greek categories of thought that were so useful to the church fathers, we shall communicate to nobody in the modern world. According to them, most of what we have inherited from the past is now out of date and no longer usable, even if it has to be retained in some formal way in order to keep the traditionalists

---

[9] Of course, neither Rome nor the Eastern Churches accepts the 'branch theory'. As far as they are concerned, what they believe is right whether others accept it or not, and thus the reunion of Christendom can only be a reabsorption of others into their church.

happy. It is not hard to see how such a view can be very appealing to some Anglicans. Just as the monarchy is no longer the power it was at the time of the Reformation, but we keep it for ceremonial purposes and it reassures those who look for continuity over time, so the Bible and the creeds can no longer be believed in the way they once were, but they provide us with a 'story' that can be adapted to meet modern needs. In practice, this approach leads to a new kind of allegory as words like 'resurrection' and 'ascension' are demythologised and recycled as psychological concepts that anyone can experience without having to tie them to historical events.

Those who think this way have a powerful voice in the modern church, especially in the developed world, where they have largely set the theological agenda over the past generation. The difficulty is that although they claim that their approach is necessary if the church is to speak to modern people, the 'modern people' they are trying to reach are not listening to them. On the contrary, wherever they have been in control the church has declined dramatically in both numbers and influence.[10] The congregations and denominations which are growing are those which reject their approach, but this embarrassment has done nothing to make them change their minds. Instead, they have often retreated from the parishes into the administrative structures of the church, creating a situation in which synods and committees are disproportionately staffed by people whose views are quite different from those held by most ordinary members on the ground. As bishops tend to be chosen from these synods and committees and not from the grass roots, the church's hierarchy is noticeably more liberal than its rank and file, a fact which has become a potential source of conflict now that parishes are being asked to bear more of the church's financial burden. Why should a conservative congregation give money to maintain a liberal bishop who (in their eyes at least) is doing more harm than good? People expect to get what they pay for and traditionalist believers, who are often very generous with their money, are not willing to pay for liberalism.

---

[10] In England for example, the high-point of the post-war revival was reached in 1963, the year in which John Robinson published his radical *Honest to God.* Numbers have been falling ever since.

In the face of such opposition, bishops and synods have a way of appealing to their status and to 'orderly procedures' in their defence, but this does not make much impression on those who believe that the hierarchy of the church is there to defend its doctrine, not to reinterpret it in the light of modern social trends. In the view of many conservatives, people in high office who cannot accept the church's official teaching ought to resign and go elsewhere. If they refuse to go of their own accord, some means should be found to remove them, or at least to allow the traditionally-minded to escape from their control. It is this belief which lies at the heart of the current crisis in the Anglican Communion. Many conservative Anglicans believe that the leadership of the American Episcopal Church and individual bishops elsewhere are not merely heretical but apostate, partly (but not exclusively) because they accept homosexual practice as legitimate, and they note that that church has seen a wave of defections from its ranks as a result.[11] Of course, critics of these defectors can always point out that the Bible says very little about homosexuality and the creeds say nothing at all, but their arguments carry little weight with the conservatives, who retort that what we are witnessing today is not a welcome outburst of freedom and creativity, but the collapse of a world-view and the wilful destruction of a culture rooted in the Bible, which is true to reality and has nourished the universal church for two thousand years. By relativising Scripture as a purely historical document and sitting light to meaning and the definition of terms, modern liberals are not only copying Humpty Dumpty, but like him, they are also heading for a fall which not even 'all the king's horses and all the king's men' will be able to put together again.

The liberal assumption that they are the ones who are in the vanguard of theological progress is also open to question. Some

---

[11] The American Episcopal Church used to be known as PECUSA (the Protestant Episcopal Church in the United States of America), though in recent years it has been customary to drop the 'Protestant' and call it simply ECUSA. In 2006 it changed its name again, this time to simply The Episcopal Church, abbreviated as TEC. To avoid confusion with other episcopal churches elsewhere, we shall refer to it as the American Episcopal Church.

of the most creative theology being done in the United Kingdom today is being done by men of a decidedly conservative outlook, like Oliver O'Donovan, Paul Helm and Richard Swinburne. Traditional Christianity retains a vitality and a fecundity which make the views of its radical opponents seem almost anaemic by comparison, even if some of it comes dressed in technical language too opaque for the non-specialist to digest! If the available evidence is anything to go by, intellectual respectability is one of the chief hallmarks of conservative Christian theology. What it lacks is not that, but a wider public sufficiently interested in it to make it a factor to be reckoned with in the church. On the one hand, the liberal élite ignores it or denounces it as 'fundamentalist', without engaging in serious dialogue with it. This is very clear if one looks at the recent book *Pierced for our transgressions*, which is a thoroughly conservative defence of the penal substitutionary doctrine of the atonement.[12] The authors are careful to quote a wide range of more liberal scholars who have written on the subject, and respond to their criticisms of the traditional doctrine in some detail. But they also point out that very often they are dealing with accusations against that doctrine which are too vaguely worded to be of much force, and that most of those who have criticised it have not bothered to engage with its more able defenders.[13] On the other hand, too many theoretically orthodox lay people and clergy are intellectually lazy and unwilling to engage with serious theology, which often strikes them as esoteric and unconnected to real life. They relate to the Bible and to public worship in an emotional, non-reflective way, which is not so much wrong as inadequate. It is true that the gospel speaks to our feelings, but it also speaks to our minds, and until a critical mass of conservative believers grasps this point the intellectual power of orthodox Christianity will not be felt in our midst. Only then will it be able to make an impression on others, whether it succeeds in converting them or not.[14]

---

[12] S. Jeffery, M. Ovey, and A. Sach, *Pierced for our transgressions* (Nottingham: IVP, 2007).
[13] *Ibid.*, pp. 325-8. See also their remarks about the non-reception of the works of the late Leon Morris on p. 26.
[14] On this point it is perhaps worth remarking that few unbelievers outside the

1.3. *The weight of history*

Every institution is shaped by its history, and the church is no exception. Whatever attitude may prevail now, there can be no doubt that the concepts of orthodoxy and heresy have shaped who and what we are. To a considerable extent, the creeds of the early church emerged because the doctrines they contain were challenged by people or groups who were denounced as heretical. Some people would argue that this process owed a good deal more to politics than to piety and that the great heretics were wrongly condemned. Whatever truth there is in that, it is fair to say that the great heresies of the ancient church have mostly died out and the theology of the creeds has been accepted on its own merits by virtually every branch of the Christian church.[15] What offends people today when they look at classical orthodoxy and the various heresies it rejected is not so much that the door was closed to alternative, or even superior ways of understanding the Christian faith, but that the orthodox pursued their victory with immoderate and un-Christian zeal.

Once Christianity became the state religion of the Roman Empire (in 380), heresy was no longer just an unacceptable theological opinion – it was a crime against the state. For over a thousand years it was taken for granted that anyone convicted of it would be punished, and in England heresy was not officially decriminalised until 1677, long after the Protestant Reformation. During the later middle ages burning at the stake was the officially approved way of eradicating it and in sixteenth-century England nearly 300 people were burnt for being Protestants. Today nobody believes that this was right, but rather than take sides, it is not uncommon for both the Reformers and their Catholic opponents to be labelled as pre-modern religious fanatics and discredited accordingly. Whether we agree with that judgment or not, we all

---

church pay any attention to the so-called 'radicals' within it. They are simply not interested in what they have to say, despite the radicals' claim that they are addressing the concerns of the modern, secular world.

[15] Some Protestant groups like the Plymouth Brethren have never accepted the creeds as such, but they affirm the theology which they contain.

recognise that the modern church has turned away from the methods it once used to deal with heresy and nobody wants to go back to them now. In some people's minds the reaction has gone so far that they want us to abandon the concept of heresy altogether and give Christians absolute freedom of expression in all circumstances – or so they claim. In practice however, not even the most radical advocates of free speech go that far. They may preach 'inclusivity', but they do not extend it to embrace racists, 'homophobes', anti-feminists or anyone who supports military intervention in places like Iraq. What is going on here is that traditional Christian doctrine is being replaced as the touchstone of orthodoxy by left-wing trendiness and political correctness. Ironically, many conservatives agree with the radicals on some or all of the above issues – where they differ from them is in their understanding of what the core of Christian belief is. For conservatives it is the Bible, not the latest popular cause, which sets the agenda for the church. The willingness of many liberals to reinterpret or disregard Scripture is just as unacceptable to them as racism. It is important to note that both sides in this debate reject any division between 'secular' and 'spiritual', but with the difference that whereas the liberals tend to dissolve the latter into the former, conservatives maintain a distinction between them. Their argument is that if people are going to do what is right in this world, then they must believe what is right in the spiritual realm that governs it. That in turn demands submission to eternal verities which may be invisible but which are no less real for that.

Another complicating factor which the reformers did not have to face is the existence of denominationalism and the modern efforts to overcome it. Until 1689, the English state did not recognise religious pluralism, and those who dissented from the official teaching of the Church of England were subject to various forms of discrimination and persecution. After 1689 there was a limited toleration granted to Protestant dissenters, and persecution virtually ceased. Even so, it was not until 1828-9 that other forms of Christianity were granted full legal rights and only much more recently has there been any serious effort to achieve reconciliation with them. Today we have grown used to welcoming Christians of other traditions as equals and most people agree that this is a good thing, but it can create problems of integrity for individual churches. For example, some Anglican ministers will not perform infant baptisms, but is the church justified in censuring them while at the same time advocating closer co-operation with Baptists? And can Baptists co-operate with Anglicans without betraying their own heritage? They originally seceded from the Church of England because they did not accept that it was a true church of Christ, but if they are now prepared to change that view, why do they continue to exist as a separate denomination? Anglicans who reject the idea of 'baptismal regeneration' share essentially the same beliefs about the sacrament as Baptists do, differing from them only over the way it is administered, so some compromise between them ought to be possible. However, there are other Anglicans who believe in baptismal regeneration and Baptists who reject the validity of any form of infant baptism, and their views cannot be so easily reconciled. The result is that we now have some Anglicans who are theologically closer to Baptists than they are to other Anglicans and Baptists who are willing to have fellowship with some Anglicans but not with others. The old labels no longer reflect theological realities on the ground, and this inevitably complicates any attempt to define what 'Anglicanism' is (or should be), let alone to exclude those who do not fit within whatever definition is arrived at.

This problem would be serious whatever the external circumstances of the church might be, but against the backdrop of a largely secularized culture, it is made worse because it seems increasingly irrelevant to most observers. Few lay Christians now identify themselves primarily in terms of their denominational affiliation, and many would happily go to a different church if it offered them what they wanted. They would probably not see this as 'desertion' or 'conversion' from one denomination to another, and might even regard the change as necessary in order for them to preserve something fundamental to their faith. For example, a communicant of the conservative Tenth Presbyterian Church in Philadelphia might become an 'Anglican' in London or Sydney where his kind of Presbyterianism is most likely to be found in an Anglican church. Similarly, an Anglican from St Helen's Bishopsgate in London might join a Presbyterian or Baptist church in the USA because the Episcopal Church there would not be congenial to him. In each case, the decision would not be based on a denominational label but on the kind of message being preached in those churches – it must be emphasised that such people would not join *any* Anglican, Presbyterian or Baptist congregation! What is going on here? The phenomenon just described is easily observed and taken for granted by those who travel for business or study reasons, but what motivates it? What is an Anglican who moves away and prefers a Presbyterian or Baptist church over the local manifestation of Anglicanism saying or implying about the local version of his own denomination?

Finally, there are also people who reject ecumenism and who are still willing to persuade Anglicans that since the Church of England (or the Anglican Communion) is hopelessly corrupt and compromised it is necessary to leave it and join a 'pure' church. At one time this 'pure' church was either Rome or one of the free church bodies, but in recent years there has been a trickle of converts to Eastern Orthodoxy as well as a blossoming of independent Evangelical congregations, often under the leadership of some charismatic individual. Of course there is movement the other way too – people from other churches become Anglicans more often than one might suppose, and there are cynics who suggest that one of the problems of the American Episcopal Church is that so many of its members are either ex-Catholics wanting sex or ex-Baptists looking for a drink![16] Should one leave the Anglican Communion on conscientious grounds, and if so, on which ones? Is the grass really greener – or the doctrine purer – on the far side of the hill? Can Anglicans seriously claim to believe something which ought to be confessed and defended? Can we honestly recommend our beliefs to others as the best way, the surest truth and the most satisfying life, or are we no more than the products of historical accidents which are frequently embarrassing, sometimes shameful and seldom if ever relevant to people today?

---

[16] What is certainly true is that the American Episcopal Church is both the least 'Anglican' member of the Anglican Communion and the one most preoccupied with defining the meaning of 'Anglicanism', a combination which bemuses Anglicans elsewhere, particularly members of the Church of England, who seldom give the matter much thought.

This booklet sets out to address these questions and others related to them, and in the process endeavours to clarify not only what we are talking about but what we should be talking about (not necessarily the same thing!) and why these questions still matter in an age of ecumenism and globalization, when 'tolerance' (which used to be a bad word) has replaced 'discrimination' (which used to be a good one) as the value most highly prized by our contemporaries, and – not coincidentally – has also recast discrimination as one of the worst vices imaginable.

2. Spiritual experience, theological orthodoxy and Anglicanism

2.1. The fundamental importance of spiritual experience

No discussion of heresy, schism or apostasy is possible without first defining what we mean by orthodoxy. Even those who believe that these concepts are now outdated have to admit that a fairly well-defined orthodoxy existed in the past, although they do not accept that it can have any controlling authority over the life of the church today. As far as they are concerned, the mentality which thought in those terms is as dead as the dodo nowadays, and those who think otherwise are little more than living fossils of a bygone era. For today's liberals 'Christianity' is a many-splendoured thing, with almost as many varieties as there are church members, and no-one has the right to impose one interpretation of it on the church to the exclusion of others. If we believe that our faith is rooted and grounded in spiritual experience alone, a conclusion of this sort is not merely unsurprising – it is virtually inevitable. My experience of God is unique to me, and if I choose to express it in unconventional ways that does not invalidate it. On the contrary, the very originality with which I express my belief may be evidence of its authenticity. After all, if I do no more than repeat the words of others, who can say whether my experience is genuine or not? We all know how easy it can be to mouth words without meaning them (or even understanding them) and we are rightly fearful of such things. Is it not far better to be honest and refuse to say what we do not believe? If we agree that it is, should we not be applauding those who have the courage to put their convictions into practice by denying traditional Christian expressions of it, instead of trying to censure them for their unbelief?

That the words we confess ought to correspond with what we have experienced seems axiomatic for the Christian. In the history of Judaeo-Christian religion, there can be no doubt that spiritual experience came before the verbal expression of it and long before that verbal expression was written down.[17] Furthermore, attempts to describe something essentially transcendent are bound to be inadequate and open to misinterpretation. We see this from the Old Testament. Abraham met with God many centuries before anyone wrote down what he said and Moses, to whom the writing of Israel's law and early traditions was attributed, had an experience of God that he could not express in human language. Whether we think of a prophet like Elijah or an apostle like Paul, the story is the same – they all had a personal encounter with God which transcended human understanding and was ultimately indescribable. What was true of them is also true of us. As Christians, we commune with God in our hearts and see him at work in our lives, but are often frustrated when trying to explain this to others because we cannot put into words what we have felt and known at a deeper level of our being. How then should we expect there to be a single confession of faith to which all Christians ought to assent as being 'true' in a way that denial of such a statement is not? How can we condemn those who, for one reason or another, are unable or unwilling to subscribe to confessional statements of this kind?

This all sounds logical and plausible, but there is another side to this argument that also has to be considered. If we make no attempt to define our experience of God, how can we know whether other people are experiencing the same God we are? Even if we cannot describe him in detail, there must be something we can say about him that will enable us to recognise him. It is only logical that if others have met him too, their experience ought to resonate with ours even if it is expressed somewhat differently. The Christian church has always claimed to be a community of faith, not just a collection of individuals who have had a spiritual experience, and so a common expression of what that faith is ought to be possible. We certainly do not want to undervalue experience

---

[17] People seldom notice it, but this is one way in which Judaism and Christianity are both quite different from Islam, where the written record is coterminous with the 'revelation'.

or suggest that it is not fundamental. The Bible says: 'Taste and see that the Lord is good', implying that those who do not experience God will never know him, and we must affirm that as strongly as we can.[18] But at the same time, we also want to insist that the God we experience exists in objective reality and that those who know him have something in common with one another.

2.1.1. *For a start, all Christians agree that any encounter we have with God must be initiated by him.*

It is quite possible to know a lot about God and even to serve him to some extent without encountering him personally. This was true of Saul of Tarsus before his conversion, and it was also true (in a different way) of the sons of Eli, who ministered in the temple during Samuel's boyhood.[19] Saul was an enthusiastic young man, well-versed in the Scriptures and in the traditions of his Jewish ancestors, and he wanted nothing more than to glorify God by promoting these things. The sons of Eli, on the other hand, although they had been trained from birth in the rituals of the tabernacle, performed them in a perfunctory manner. In stark contrast to the enthusiasm of Saul of Tarsus, their hearts were not in what they were doing and their behaviour contradicted what they officially represented. Both types of people are common today, and there are even cases of young enthusiasts like Saul turning into old cynics like the sons of Eli! But despite their different circumstances, neither Saul nor the sons of Eli had a personal encounter with God until he came to them. Saul was struck down on the road to Damascus and forced to recognise the lordship of the Christ whom he had been persecuting.[20] The sons of Eli were less fortunate, because when God came to them it was to punish their wickedness and bring their family to an end. As individuals, they were no worse than Saul and their petty corruption was probably less harmful to God's people than Saul's persecution was. But God came to save the one and condemn the others for reasons known only to him. So it has always been. The prophets of the Old

---

[18] Psalm 34:8.
[19] See Philippians 3:4-6 and 1 Samuel 2:12-36.
[20] Acts 9: 1-9.

Testament were handpicked by God, often against their own will. Few went as far as Jonah in their attempts to run away, but his story merely confirms how fundamental God's call is. When God comes into our lives, there can be no escape from him.

In the New Testament Jesus picked his own disciples, including Judas, whom he knew would eventually betray him. We do not know why this was so, and neither did anyone else at the time. One of the most unsettling episodes in the Gospels is the story of the Last Supper, when Jesus reveals that one of his disciples would betray him and each of them wondered whether he would be the guilty one.[21] Even at that late hour, none of them could say which way he would turn when put to the test! There were others who wanted to follow Jesus during the course of his earthly ministry, but they were rebuffed. The rich young ruler seemed like an ideal disciple, but when he was challenged to give up all his possessions, he failed the test because he had not been chosen for discipleship.[22] Others sought leave to sort out their affairs before committing themselves, but they were sent away because they were unfit for the kingdom of God.[23] Later on we find the Apostle Paul saying that the Corinthian church was composed of 'the foolish things of this world' because God had chosen them to shame the wise.[24] It is much the same today. Recently a clerk working for British Airways, a humble lady called Nadia Edeewa, was suspended from her job because she insisted on wearing a cross around her neck in honour of Jesus. A furore ensued and Miss Edeewa was eventually vindicated, but not before Richard Dawkins, an Oxford professor and militant atheist, remarked that hers was 'the stupidest face' he had ever seen. Professor Dawkins did not know it, but in saying this he was describing a saint – one of God's foolish ones, chosen by him to bring shame on the wise and powerful of this world.[25]

It often happens that we come across books written by

---

[21] Matthew 26:22.
[22] Mark 10:17-22.
[23] Luke 9:57-62.
[24] 1 Corinthians 1:18-31.
[25] 1 Corinthians 1:27.

people who have gone in search of God. Some of these people have failed to find him and have admitted as much, but others have found spiritual satisfaction in different ways and have chosen to put what they have found in place of God in their lives. Many of these stories are deeply moving, and there is no reason to doubt their authors' sincerity, but whatever they have found, it is not the God of the Bible. Like it or not, they have come up with an idol, a subjective creation of their own minds which they have configured to suit themselves. Almost invariably the god of their imagination turns out to be much nicer and more user-friendly that the one who reveals himself in Scripture. More often than not he is a loving being who accentuates everything positive in human life and ignores whatever is unpleasant or negative. He is almost never a God of wrath or punishment and so it is not uncommon for these people to claim that he is much to be preferred to the God of the Bible, whose politically incorrect wrath remains on those who do not believe in him.[26]

Other people make a serious effort to discover the principle underlying the universe and are happy to talk about a 'supreme being' or an 'ultimate reality', but find it difficult to think of this in personal terms. Their ideal is something to be honoured and respected, but it cannot be compared to a Father in heaven who wants to be loved and obeyed. Christians can understand the attraction of such views and see in them some similarity to our own beliefs, but however noble and upright these seekers after truth may be, they are not Christians. Despite all their searching, they have not found the well-spring of eternal life. Instead, they too have created an idol in their minds, a refined and exalted idol no doubt, but still a creature of their imagination to whom we cannot bow down and whom we cannot serve.

The God of the Bible comes to us as a personal being, with all the complexity that personal relationships involve. He cannot be simplified into an abstract set of ideas, nor can he be identified with anything he has created, however magnificent that creation

---

[26] John 3:36. For a good example of someone who does this, see K. Ward, *Rethinking Christianity* (Oxford: Oneworld, 2007).

might be. He comes to us as a God of love, but he is also a God who punishes those who rebel against him, and there is no contradiction in this. He brings us eternal life, but he also tells us that we must die to this world in order to obtain it. Moreover, it often seems that death is more immediate and painful than the promised eternity which remains stubbornly hidden from our eyes, and this is the great challenge we face as believers. To walk in faith is to know a God whose ways are past finding out, even when we understand enough of them to be able to take the next step forward. As Jesus said to Nicodemus: 'We speak of what we know and bear witness to what we have seen.' Then he adds: "But you do not receive our testimony.'[27] Only a personal encounter with God could have persuaded Nicodemus that Jesus was right, but only by being born again by his Holy Spirit can any one receive his testimony. This new birth must come from God, whose Spirit blows wherever he wills.[28] Scandalous as it seems to many, there is no other way to know him, and Christians do no-one any favours by pretending otherwise.

2.1.2.   *Secondly, all Christians agree that the most important mark of the believer is a spirit of humble obedience in the presence of God and his Word.*

The Apostle Paul did not hesitate to tear a strip off those whom he accused of perverting the gospel message and he routinely denounced those who questioned his Apostolic authority, yet towards the end of his life he was able to tell the Ephesian Christians:

> Of this gospel I was made a minister according to the gift of God's grace, which was given me by the working of his power. To me, though I am the very least of all the saints, this grace was

---

[27] John 3:11.

[28] John 3:7-8. All Christians agree about this, but Evangelical Protestants differ from Roman Catholics and Eastern Orthodox by refusing to accept that the new birth automatically occurs in baptism. Too many people have been baptised without showing any sign of spiritual regeneration for such an identification to be plausible, and in any case, it cannot be true that spiritual rebirth is subject to human action – and therefore also to human manipulation.

given, to preach to the Gentiles the unsearchable riches of Christ...[29]

It is all too easy in a hierarchical and establishment-minded church like ours to think that a university professor or a bishop possesses some kind of special knowledge and authority deriving from his studies and position. But history shows that those who have made the deepest impression on the church have often been relatively humble people whom God has raised up for the task – men like William Tyndale, John Wesley and Charles Simeon. They were not ignoramuses (neither was Paul!) but they were not intellectuals either, and they were certainly not members of the church's hierarchy. It is true that there have been godly bishops whose influence has outlasted their time, including Anglicans like Thomas Cranmer and John Charles Ryle, and in the early church, most of the leading theologians and preachers held episcopal office, though in many cases this meant little more than it would mean today to be the pastor of a large congregation. Unfortunately, it must also be said that few Anglican bishops have been particularly memorable and some have been downright scandalous. On balance, most of them have done their job reasonably well but have left little trace, which is perhaps as it should be. Exceptions like Cranmer and Ryle are remembered today not because of their earthly status, but because of their devotion to God – for them to live was Christ, and to die was gain.[30] It is this, and not their worldly attainments or success, that has marked them out as voices that continue to echo across the centuries.

Humility is never an easy virtue to learn, but if a hierarchical church has problems with this, they are as nothing compared with the world of academe. There the problem is compounded because a university professor is expected to discover new things and come up with new ideas, an expectation that sits uneasily with the essential givenness of theology. Christians believe that God has revealed himself once for all in Jesus Christ

---

[29] Ephesians 3:7-8.
[30] Philippians 1:21.

and so there is nothing fundamentally new to discover. Of course the revelation is complex and incomplete, and in the constantly changing circumstances of the world around us our faith has to be continually explored and reformulated. But even so, originality and new discoveries of the kind common in the natural sciences are essentially alien to the discipline. When we hear prominent theologians claim that what we have always believed is wrong and must be substantially modified or abandoned, we must be extremely cautious. There may be something in what they say, and if we have expressed our beliefs inadequately in the past we must adapt our language in the light of new understanding. A good example of this is the way in which the image and likeness of God in human beings has been misunderstood.[31] Greek thinkers supposed that the use of two different words meant that there must be two different things, and concluded that at the fall, Adam and Eve lost the likeness of God but retained his image. On that basis they were able to present salvation as the restoration of God's likeness to an image that was otherwise still intact. At the time of the Reformation, scholars who learned Hebrew realised that 'image' and 'likeness' were two different words for the same thing. They still had to account for the fall, of course, and so they said that Adam and Eve lost the image/likeness at the fall. This meant that fallen human beings had no foundation of godliness on which the grace of God could operate; any likeness to God in us had to be introduced by him *ex nihilo*. In fact however, the Bible does not say that the image and likeness of God were lost at the fall, and it is clear from subsequent passages that they were retained.[32] As a result, the fall of man cannot be regarded as a corruption or loss of the image and likeness of God, but has to be explained in some other way.

This discovery will strike some people as 'new' because they have not realised it before, but it is not really new at all – it has been there in the Bible all along and simply overlooked or misunderstood. Moreover, modern theologians who understand this have not created a new orthodoxy which contradicts the fathers

---

[31] Genesis 1:26-7.
[32] See Genesis 9:6; James 3:9.

of the church or the Reformers. What is constant in the history of Christian thought is the belief that the human race has been created with a likeness to God not enjoyed by any other creature and that through its own disobedience it has fallen away from that ideal. Changes in the way the image and likeness of God have been understood have not altered these fundamental facts, but merely caused them to be expressed in a different way. Theologians have a lot of work to do in correcting mistakes like this, but they do so by expounding the Scriptures more accurately, not by making new discoveries which overturn the way we look at God and his work of salvation.

Unfortunately, it often seems to be the case that academic theologians are not interested in illuminating the truth of the gospel but in shocking those whom they regard as simple (and therefore simplistic) believers. Some of them have claimed that the incarnation of Christ is a 'myth', whatever they mean by that, and others have said that the bones of Jesus may be lying about somewhere in Palestine. Esoteric texts recovered from the sands of Egypt, like the so-called *Gospel of Judas*, are adduced as evidence that the four canonical Gospels are wrong or inadequate. Serious scholars know that such claims are false, but their balanced and nuanced approach seldom gets a hearing.[33] Instead, the general public learns only that professor so-and-so or the bishop of x-place does not believe the Bible. The sad thing is that although the popular press exaggerates this phenomenon, it is seldom completely wrong – after all is said and done, it is usually true that the professors and bishops they like to quote are not traditional Christian believers and are out to attack the beliefs of those who are. Even worse, they show no sign of humility about their claims, nor do they regret upsetting non-specialists by their incautious remarks. No doubt it is always possible to find mindless and ignorant church members, but the attitude which these prominent people betray towards others is a long way from the charity expected of a Christian leader. Jesus came into the world in great humility, and the Apostle Paul willingly suffered all kinds of

---

[33] For a good and clear examination of the most recent claims, see Darrell L. Bock, *The missing Gospels* (Nashville: Nelson, 2006).

privation and abuse for the sake of the gospel. When we hear voices making loud claims about what those men said but showing no sign of the spiritual grace which accompanied their message we must turn away, because what they are saying, even if it contains an element of truth, amounts in the end to a denial of the gospel.

2.1.3.   *Thirdly, all Christians believe that although we can know who God is and what he is like, we can never know everything about him.*

An illustration may help to explain what this means. I sometimes meet people who knew my parents when they were younger, and they tell me things that I never knew about them or else perceive differently from the way I do. I have learned a lot about my parents in this way, but even if they say things about them that I have never heard before, I can still recognize whether they are telling the truth about them or not. For example, if one of them were to say that he knew my father when he was a subsistence farmer in Afghanistan, I would know he was not telling the truth – and could prove it. If another one said that my father was often drunk and beat my mother, I might find it hard to disprove the allegation but I would sense that it was untrue from personal experience and would not trust my so-called 'informant'. If a third one claimed that my mother used to walk her dog in the park behind her house I would know that it was untrue, because there is no park behind her house and she does not have a dog. In this last example, the first element is certain and demonstrable, and the second I know to be true from my own experience, though perhaps she had a dog before I was born and I never knew about it.

Sometimes the truth turns out to be more complicated that we might think. Most of my father's old friends believe that he was the eldest of twelve children and take it for granted that I will agree with them, but although I understand what they mean and accept it as far as it goes, I know that what they believe is not strictly true. My father was actually the third of fifteen children, but because the first two and the seventh died in infancy, most of his friends think he was the eldest of twelve. In this case I normally accept as 'true' something I know to be false, mainly because it makes little difference one way or the other and there is little point in disabusing these people of their belief. But another reason I seldom correct these people is that when I have done so in the past they have often told me that I was wrong. They point out that they knew my father and his family when they were growing up and I did not, so how can I claim to know more than they do about them? Surely their eye-witness testimony is to be preferred to mine, which is only oral tradition handed down to the next generation! Perhaps so, but I know that I am right and they are wrong because I have heard it on authority – from my grandmother. As she was in a position to know, I believe her and not my father's friends and I am convinced that if I ever had to prove it, the documentation can be found in some record office or other. I have not seen it or gone to look for it but I believe it is there and that I could dig it out if I had to.

Our knowledge of God our heavenly Father is in many ways comparable to this. We can learn a great deal about him from other people, and frequently do. We appreciate that others see and experience him in ways different from us. But there are some things people say about God that we know are wrong, whether we can demonstrate it objectively or not. They may be factually untrue, as for example, when people say that Jesus did not rise from the dead. They may be false value judgments, as when people suggest that God cannot be loving because he punishes some people for their wickedness and sends them to hell. There may be complications in our knowledge that require further investigation if they are to be properly understood. For example, many Christians find it difficult to explain precisely how Jesus is related to God the Father. If there is only one God, how can Jesus be God too? A common response to this is to say that the Father is God in the absolute sense and that Jesus is God's Son, closely related to the Father but somehow not quite the same as he is. Beyond that, they are at a loss. Popular reluctance to call Jesus God often stems from a fear that it might compromise monotheism, which is of fundamental importance for our faith. It is not easy to find an acceptable way to express Christ's divinity without endangering belief in the one God, and it took the church a long time to arrive at an acceptable solution to this problem. On the way there were many false starts and inadequate statements, which were finally resolved by what we now call the doctrine of the Trinity. There is no denying that the Trinity is hard for many people to understand

and that there is a strong temptation to simplify things in the way sketched out above. The result is an unsophisticated form of the great fourth-century heresy known as Arianism, which claimed that the Son was a divine creature who was born at some point in time.[34] Arianism is the wrong answer to the problem of Christ's divinity, but most people who fall into it (or something like it) do so innocently – they are trying to explain something they instinctively know about but which is beyond their ability to explain. What they end up with is a heresy but it would be wrong to call them heretics because they have not done this intentionally or even knowingly; it is ignorance, not malice or rejection which has led them into error. We expect that when the intricacies of the doctrine are properly explained to them, they will assent to the truth, even if they still find it hard to understand. There is biblical precedent for this in the case of Apollos, a Jew from Alexandria who preached the gospel of Christ but knew only the baptism of John. When he was corrected by Priscilla and Aquila, he accepted what they had to say and went on to become a powerful witness to Christ.[35]

2.2. *Why spiritual experience is not enough*

Personal experience plays an important part in our faith, but as the example I gave of my father and his friends demonstrates, it also has its limitations. Experience is seldom completely wrong, but it needs to be supplemented by a higher understanding which can put it in context and make sense of it. Christians accept the testimony of the prophets and apostles because they were given that understanding and authorised by God to explain it to us. There were plenty of eye-witnesses to the life and death of Jesus, but what they learned about him by observation still left them trying to guess whether he was the promised Messiah or not. Even his mother and the disciples who lived with him failed to understand who he was or what he had come to do.[36] Jesus could not be figured out by

---

[34] Arius (256-336) was a presbyter at Alexandria who was accused of saying this about the year 318.
[35] Acts 18:24-28.
[36] This point is made quite clearly in John 14:8-10.

observation alone, no matter how intensive it was. It was only by revelation from a higher authority that the disciples came to appreciate the truth, and it was on the basis of that authority that they preached it to the world after Jesus had ascended into heaven.[37]

Thanks to the revelation given to them, the prophets and apostles are the human foundations of the church.[38] The process by which the spiritual experiences of the ancient Israelites came to be written down and preserved is largely unknown to us, but it was undoubtedly the work of many people who were responding to the inspiration of great spiritual leaders whom God raised up from time to time. There were schools of prophets whose words were recorded by temple scribes and shaped into the texts that we know today.[39] By the time of Jesus their work was largely complete and had been accepted by the Jewish community, though not without some cost. There had already been a split in the nation which had produced the Samaritans, a group which accepted the Jewish law but challenged the legitimacy of the temple worship at Jerusalem and were therefore ostracised by orthodox Jews.[40] Jesus had a more positive view of the Samaritans and could portray them in a favourable light, as least as individuals, but when it came to the basic principles of the faith, he was firmly on the Jewish side and said so.[41]

There were other divisions in the Jewish community which did not lead to open division, most notably the one between the conservative Pharisees and the more 'liberal' Sadducees.[42] Jesus had a low opinion of both of them, but for different reasons. He criticised the Pharisees mainly for their behaviour, which reflected

---

[37] See Matthew 16:13-19.
[38] Ephesians 2:20.
[39] There are many theories about how this occurred, but no-one can say for sure – all we have to go on are the texts themselves, most of which have come down to us only in their final form.
[40] John 4:9.
[41] See Luke 10:25-37 and John 4:22.
[42] The Sadducees were more 'liberal' because they denied the resurrection of the body and were more open to Hellenistic influences.

a false interpretation of the Jewish law. Instead of seeing it as a spiritual gift, they had turned it into a literalistic code, and when they found it impossible to observe as it stood, they reinterpreted it in ways which made it more bearable.[43] Jesus regarded this as hypocrisy and condemned it accordingly. With the Sadducees however, he disagreed doctrinally and did not hesitate to tell them that they did not understand either the Scriptures or the power of God.[44] The Sadducees' mistake was more serious than that of the Pharisees, because whereas the latter merely had to correct their behaviour, the former had to change their fundamental beliefs. This may be one reason why we hear more about the Pharisees in the New Testament than about other forms of Judaism – for all their faults, they were closer to the truth than the others were.

Nevertheless, acceptance of Christianity meant rejection of all forms of Judaism, a painful separation which still affects us today. The history of Judaeo-Christian relations is an unhappy one, and Christians must repent of their past attitudes and behaviour towards Jews. But we cannot take this to the point of saying that Judaism is an acceptable alternative to Christianity or that Jews do not need Christ as their Saviour. That would be denying the clear witness of the New Testament, most of which was written by Jews who were trying to evangelise their own people. We cannot pretend that Judaism is a valid way of salvation which we have simply misunderstood. If we are followers of Jesus we are obliged to say, as the Apostle Paul and the first generation of Christians said, that the Law of Moses has been superseded by the gospel. To say this is not to insult or disparage Jews, but to honour them as the people to whom the message of the Saviour was first given and to encourage them to claim their own spiritual inheritance in Christ.

As the early church began to grow it soon became apparent that there were different kinds of spiritual experience within it and many false teachers purporting to be messengers sent by God. In that situation, the Apostles had to record the true gospel so that those who had not witnessed the historical events would be able to

---

[43] See Mark 7:9-13.
[44] Matthew 22:29.

distinguish fact from fantasy. The result was the New Testament, which remains the supreme authority for Christian belief. The Apostles and their assistants were inspired by God to produce reliable accounts of the life and teaching of Jesus and to define the gospel in an authoritative way. Their purpose was not to suppress individual spiritual experience but to examine it and discern whether it was of God or not. Anyone who claimed to have a revelation or teaching which did not agree with theirs was to be rejected, a point on which the New Testament is very clear.[45] It has become fashionable in modern scholarship to say that the first churches contained people of widely different beliefs and that what we think of today as 'orthodoxy' was imposed only gradually. There is some truth in this, as the New Testament makes plain. Where this theory is mistaken is in its assumption that the wide variety was tolerated and that in the early days of the church everyone's opinion was given more-or-less equal status. A glance at the New Testament epistles will show that the apostles wrote to their churches in order to correct errors, not to dialogue with them or find a workable compromise between competing factions on points of doctrine. It is true that Paul advised discretion when dealing with the tender consciences of those who found it difficult to embrace the full implications of the gospel, but the circumstances in which he did this have to be borne in mind. When Paul told people not to eat meat which had been sacrificed to idols because of the offence it might cause to some Jewish Christians, he was quite clear about the underlying theological principles – everything God has made is good, idols do not exist, and in principle there is nothing wrong with eating meat that has been sacrificed to them. But there were some people who thought that eating such meat was showing honour to a pagan cult when they were trying to distance themselves from such things. For their sakes, Paul advised Christians not to eat meat sacrificed to idols even though there was nothing wrong with it in itself.[46] Believers could always find something else to eat and it was not worth alienating the weaker brethren for something of no real importance. Practical

---

[45] See Galatians 1:8-9; 2 Peter 2:1-3; 1 John 4:1-6; Jude 4.
[46] 1 Corinthians 8:1-13; Romans 14:13-23.

compassion of this kind is not the same as compromise on matters of principle, something that Paul never contemplated.

2.3. The emergence of orthodoxy

Later on, the church was forced to determine what the Bible's teaching was on any number of issues, ranging from the creation of the world to the last judgment. The basic outlines of what Scripture said were clear enough, but there were many subtleties which had to be teased out and it took several centuries for this to be done adequately. For instance, did God create the world out of nothing or out of some unformed matter which had previously existed? To the superficial eye, the Genesis account suggests that God worked on unformed matter, but where did that matter come from? Everything that exists is in God's power and Paul tells us that he created everything,[47] so the answer must be that he created the world out of nothing. Decisions like this one were not taken by individuals but by church councils which were summoned for the purpose. Not all of these councils came to the right conclusions but those that erred were not ratified by the church and are no longer recognised as authoritative. Along with almost all Western Christians, Anglicans have always accepted that the decisions taken by the first four 'ecumenical' councils are faithful to the teaching of Scripture and have regarded them as forming part of the inheritance of orthodoxy.[48] We also accept the decisions of the fifth and sixth councils, though not the canons which were later associated with them.[49] We have had more difficulty with the

---

[47] Eph. 3:9.

[48] These were the first council of Nicaea (325), the first council of Constantinople (381), the first council of Ephesus (431), the council of Chalcedon (451). Their legal standing in the Church of England derives from the old canon law, which is still in force to the extent that it has not been repealed. See D 15, cc. 1-3 in *Corpus iuris canonici*, ed. E. Friedberg (2 vols., Graz: Akademische Verlag, 1995), I, 34-41. (This is a reprint of the edition of 1879.)

[49] The second council of Constantinople (553) and the third council of Constantinople (680-1). The canons connected with them were passed by the Eastern church only at a council held in Constantinople in 691-2. They were not accepted in the west because of the way they delegitimised certain western practices, like the use of unleavened bread in the eucharist. For their authority in

seventh council, which was held at Nicaea in 787 and is recognised by both the Roman Catholic and the Eastern Orthodox churches. That council met to decide whether the historical fact of the incarnation of Christ made it permissible to paint pictures of Jesus. On the theological point at issue, we agree with the council's positive conclusion – Jesus was visible to his disciples and therefore it must be possible to depict him. However, we are less happy with the conclusion that such pictures must not only be made but also venerated. The New Testament says nothing about this and gives us no clue as to what Jesus looked like. We therefore reject those decisions of this council that enjoin practices which are plainly 'repugnant to the Word of God'.[50] Similar considerations apply to later councils of the Western church, which we do not regard as infallible but which we are prepared to accept to the extent that they reflect biblical teaching.[51]

At the time of the Reformation, the Church of England did its best to root out rites and ceremonies which were being abused by superstitious people, and claimed the freedom to decide what could and could not be done in worship, as long as it did not contravene anything in Scripture.[52] Some people thought it should go further and accept only those rites and ceremonies which could claim some kind of biblical precedent, but this was not practically possible and was rejected by the majority. Those who continued to insist on that principle came to be known as Puritans, and eventually many of them left the Church of England. It should however be noted that those who conformed to the established church did not differ on any significant point of doctrine from the non-conformist Puritans. What divided them was the way in which that doctrine should be applied in practice. That this should have led to permanent division is tragic, but we who have remained 'conformists' and now claim the name 'Anglican' must recognise that *in theological terms* many of those on the other side of this

---

the Church of England, see D 16 cc. 6-8 (Friedberg, I, 43-5).
[50] Article 22. For the detailed Anglican argument, see the second homily in the Second Book of Homilies, entitled 'Against peril of idolatry'.
[51] Article 21.
[52] Articles 20 and 34.

divide are one with us in matters of faith. The Puritan devotional and theological heritage is Anglican as much as it is Presbyterian or Baptist and none of us would spurn Richard Baxter or John Bunyan simply because they were at odds with the establishment.

What is easy to overlook in the history of Christian doctrine, though it becomes clear once it is pointed out, is that no individual has ever been given the authority to determine what orthodoxy is.[53] At the time of the Reformation, Anglican apologists liked to compare their monarchs to the rulers of ancient Israel – King Edward VI was the new Josiah, Queen Elizabeth I the new Deborah, and so on. Even the clergy were compared to the priests and Levites in the temple, particularly when it came to justifying the payment of tithes to support them! But if the kings and priests did not do their job properly, they could be dispensed with, as happened on more than one occasion in the first two centuries after the Reformation. Bishops were expected to uphold Christian doctrine and enforce the church's discipline within their dioceses, but they had no authority to change or to dissent from them. It was exactly the same for professors of theology in the universities. All of them had to subscribe to the Thirty-nine Articles of Religion and swear that they would uphold the official teaching of the church. If they failed to do so they could be censured and deprived of their office.[54] Like bishops and parish clergy, theologians were regarded as ministers of the church and could not claim the right to alter or to reject its beliefs. No-one has ever claimed that we know everything there is to know about God, but we hang onto what we do know because it is on that knowledge that our salvation depends. What we are not told in the Bible is not essential for that. The church permits us to speculate on other matters, but does not (and cannot) demand that we should assent to things that are not revealed to us in Scripture.

---

[53] The doctrine of papal infallibility was not proclaimed until 1870 and is a genuine aberration as far as the earlier tradition is concerned.
[54] This happened as late as 1710 to William Whiston of Cambridge. He denied the Trinity and was forced out of the university because of it.

2.4.   The church and its teachers

The New Testament tells us that some people are given more theological understanding than others. All Christians are equal in the sight of God, but some have been chosen to become teachers of his people.[55] God has equipped them with the aptitude and intelligence needed to probe the difficult parts of his self-revelation through the prophets and apostles, not so that they can be an advanced élite lording it over the rest of us but so that they can serve the church by using their knowledge and skills for the benefit of everyone.

In developing the theme of Christian ministry Paul uses the image of the body. We all have bodies and most of us know something about the way they work. We have a fairly good idea of what causes pain, of how to deal with most ordinary symptoms and of what we need to do in order to keep going from one day to the next. But there are many things about our bodies that we do not know and cannot do anything about, and here we have to rely on specialists who have dedicated their lives to studying them. At one level a doctor is no better than anyone else, and a wise physician will always make sure that his patients are co-operating with him as far as possible. Only the patients know where they are hurting, and a good doctor has to teach them to express this as accurately as possible, so as to make it easier for him to treat them.

It is the same with a good theologian. Theologians are the doctors of the soul, men who have studied the mysteries of God in as much depth as they have been revealed to us, and who are equipped to help us develop a greater understanding of him. If theologians are doing their job properly, they are listening to God's people as much as instructing them. Even the best principles mean little if they are not properly applied, and it is only church members who can tell them what their problems are. Just as doctor and patient must work together for healing, so theologian and believer have to co-operate if real results are to be achieved.[56]

---

[55] See 1 Corinthians 12: 28-29; Ephesians 4:11.
[56] It follows from this that theologians must be involved with God's people and

34

Ultimately, the success of the theologian is not determined by the cleverness of his diagnosis but by the health of the members of the body of Christ in his care, and it is in this context that heresy becomes a particularly sensitive issue.

In the medical field there is no-one more dangerous than the quack who thinks he knows what to do but lacks the training needed to understand the effects of his actions. Quacks cannot be wiped out completely because there will always be some people who prefer home-made remedies to professional advice, and real doctors can do no more than warn people against this kind of thing. It is the same with theology. There will always be amateurs who think they have all the answers, and true theologians can only warn people off them. If the spiritual quacks have charismatic personalities, as they often do, they are quite likely to attract a considerable following and there is not much that can be done about it, though we still have to try, knowing that the charisma will eventually fade but solid teaching will endure from one generation to the next.

Beyond this there lies another danger which has largely been overcome in the medical profession but is a major problem in theology. Until the nineteenth century anyone who consulted a physician was taking his life in his hands, because most doctors were practising their profession in the wrong way. Their offices were full of potions and equipment of different kinds, but these were often applied without any scientific basis and it is a wonder that any of the patients survived their treatment. Today this problem has largely been put right and it would be a major scandal if anyone were to revive the practices of the eighteenth century. Unfortunately, in the theological sphere, almost the exact opposite development has occurred. At the very time when medicine was being put on a solid foundation, theology was being dislodged from the one it had in the Bible. Instead of being gifted expositors of the sacred text, many theologians became cut-price philosophers, more

---

active in his church. The Bible knows nothing of 'ivory tower' theology, and neither should we. One of Karl Barth's greatest contributions to our understanding was his insistence that good theology must be preached and preachable!

35

prone to scepticism than to faith and dissecting their source material with the kind of zeal they should have been reserving for protecting the souls of their flocks. As a result, modern theology has fallen into the kind of anarchy which characterized pre-modern medicine. Even if its practitioners cannot be called quacks, their failure to ground their discipline in its only scientifically reliable source, Holy Scripture, has produced much the same result. Just as the sufferer who entered an eighteenth-century hospital was in danger of losing his life, so the theological student who enters a modern faculty of theology is in danger of losing his soul, because many of those currently regarded as masters of the discipline do not understand their subject matter and mishandle it.

Fortunately the picture is not all doom and gloom and we must be grateful that we have inherited a large body of excellent teaching which has come down to us through the centuries. We should not idolize the past unduly but we must recognise that it has left us a large body of solid theology that can still be of great comfort and assistance to us today. No doubt there were just as many bad theologians in the middle ages or during the Reformation period as there are now, but over time they have faded into the background and been forgotten, whereas the good ones have survived and proved their worth from one generation to the next.[57] Some church historians like to point out that the creeds and confessions we think of as standard were produced by fallible men who were not averse to using underhanded tactics to achieve their aims, and we must admit that there is some truth in this. The church has never been perfect and even the greatest saints have had their weaknesses. What matters is not the fallibility of particular individuals but the long-term survival of their work.[58] Even if every bishop at the first council of Nicaea in AD 325 had been bribed to vote against Arius (which was not the case) that would not invalidate the condemnation itself, because it was upheld in later times by people acting with no such prompting, and it is still being defended today. Perhaps the truth was sometimes

---

[57] Even the great heretics of the past are known to us mainly through the works written against them by their orthodox opponents.

[58] This is not to excuse their fallibility, but rather to leave judgment to God.

arrived at by dubious means, but it has survived the circumstances in which it was first formulated and continues to inspire and inform us today.

Modern theology is a different matter altogether. Here we have to deal with each new work as it comes off the press and make some assessment of it before it has been tried and tested. Those who did their theological studies thirty or so years ago will recall the great names of that era – Don Cupitt, Maurice Wiles, Geoffrey Lampe, John Robinson and so on. But where are they now? The truth is that they have been forgotten for the most part, because what they had to say was of no value to the church and has been rejected. When we go back a bit further, we see this phenomenon even more clearly. It is now just over a century since Albert Schweitzer published his classic work, *The quest for the historical Jesus*, in which he demolished the theories of virtually every major New Testament scholar in nineteenth-century Europe. Schweitzer attacked the great men of his day, but the most interesting thing about his book is how few of those names mean anything to us, because almost all of them have disappeared into oblivion. Yet for Schweitzer and his contemporaries they were the leading lights of the time – after all, no-one would bother demolishing the theories of nonentities!

When we look at the Anglican world of the nineteenth century, there were many prominent liberal theologians who seemed at the time to be carrying all before them – Benjamin Jowett, for example, or Charles Gore, to name but two. Yet the only Anglican theologian of that era whose works are still being published and read today is the conservative Evangelical John Charles Ryle, the first bishop of Liverpool (1880-1900). Ryle's works have never been read by the theological 'mainstream' which continues to ignore them, but they still sell in respectable quantities and are widely read by serious pastors and students all over the world. By contrast, Jowett and Gore are known only to specialists and to students doing a course on the Victorian church, who soon forget about them after they graduate.

Moreover, there are still gifted theologians who honour and expound the tradition which has come down to us from biblical times and who eschew any quest for novelty for its own sake.

Traditionalism has acquired a negative connotation in many circles, but there is no reason why the orthodoxy which lies behind it should not be a living, vibrant and dynamic expression of the Christian faith today. Perhaps some traditionalists are pedantic bores who are mired in a golden age that never was, but this must not blind us to the fact that there are true exponents of the tradition who are as lively, provocative and stimulating now as their predecessors were many centuries ago and whose work is far more exciting than anything liberalism has to offer. Anyone who doubts this need only look at the writings of Colin Gunton (Reformed), Thomas Weinandy (Roman Catholic) or John Zizioulas (Eastern Orthodox) to see how true this is. Among Anglicans, the works of men like C. S. Lewis, James Packer and John Stott continue to outsell those of the liberal establishment *put together*, for the simple reason that these men know God in a way that their liberal rivals do not. The academy may not honour them, but the general public knows what it wants and demonstrates it by keeping their books at the top of the best-seller lists from one year to the next.

Orthodox Christian theology is not the exclusive property of any one denomination or spiritual tradition. It is alive and well across the entire spectrum of Christian belief and those who walk with Christ recognise it wherever it appears. As Anglicans we are children of the Protestant Reformation and grateful for that inheritance, but this does not stop us from welcoming a godly Roman Catholic when we meet one or from learning from his insights into the mysteries of God. We are happy to look anywhere for good teaching, and will learn just as readily from a Baptist like Donald Carson as from an Orthodox like Anthony Bloom. This is not because we are indifferent to matters of truth and doctrine, but because we recognize that the Spirit of God is at work in many people who disagree with us in some ways but who are one with us in the essentials of the faith. At the same time, we do not hesitate to reject fellow Anglicans if they do not reflect the work of the Holy Spirit in their lives. Some of them may be great powers in the church at the moment, but their influence on the godly is nil and past experience suggests that a generation from now they will have been completely forgotten.

2.5. Catholic orthodoxy and Anglicanism

Catholic orthodoxy is the teaching of Holy Scripture as this has been summarized in the great creeds of the Christian church and in the decisions taken at the ancient ecumenical councils.[59] Orthodox catholicity recognizes the presence of this teaching in every Christian church, from the Plymouth Brethren at one end of the spectrum to the Eastern Orthodox at the other, without suggesting that any one of these churches possesses the truth in a special or exclusive sense.[60] Spiritual truth cannot be controlled by a visible structure or institution; it will always be too great for that. In this sense traditional Anglican 'comprehensiveness' is a genuine virtue for which we must be grateful, because it means that Anglicans can go anywhere in the Christian world and be welcomed as long as we concentrate on what C. S. Lewis called 'mere Christianity'. At its best, Anglicanism can claim to be the most balanced and the most ecumenical expression of Christianity which exists in the modern world. It is catholic orthodoxy and orthodox catholicity incarnated in the visible structure of a church that manages to retain its solidity without losing its flexibility and openness to those of other traditions.

We must make no apology for this. At the heart of Christianity lies the Bible, which dominates our thinking and influences the Anglican inheritance to an extraordinary degree. Despite all the fissiparous tendencies of English-speaking Protestantism, the Bible has held us together – the work of King James and his committees has proved its worth and has been accepted by everyone, regardless of their particular theological or

---

[59] It is true that there are some loose ends here which ought to be recognized. For example, the Eastern Orthodox churches do not accept the double procession of the Holy Spirit from the Father 'and the Son' as the Western version of the Nicene Creed states it, and there are also great churches of the east which have not received the teaching of the council of Chalcedon (AD 451) which is so fundamental to the Christological thinking of the rest of Christendom. However, it is now generally agreed that the real problem in both cases is one of formulation rather than of substance, and that on the essential points, all traditional Christian churches are in substantial agreement.
[60] In this respect we often differ from these churches themselves!

ecclesiastical preferences.[61] Today, virtually nobody engages in denominational Bible study or sectarian Bible translation and those who do, like the Jehovah's Witnesses, are almost always heretical cults that are not recognised as Christian. The Bible is the most ecumenical standard of doctrine we possess and faithfulness to its teaching remains the touchstone of faithfulness to Christ, whatever denominational label we wear.

To say that the Anglican tradition is based on the Bible may seem obvious enough to some, but in modern times this has been qualified by a school of thought which has tried to insist that *sola Scriptura* is not the touchstone of true Anglicanism. Instead, they say that Anglicans typically believe in a three-fold cord of Scripture, tradition and reason which are complementary authorities. This idea is supposed to go back to Richard Hooker (1554-1600) whom they have elevated to the status of being the classical exponent of Anglicanism. This reconstruction of Anglicanism has been particularly influential in the United States where it has spawned a whole generation of scholars and theologians dedicated to expounding it in these terms. It is all the more interesting therefore to read the recent book by Professor Rowan Greer, Emeritus Professor of Anglican Studies at Yale University, entitled *Anglican approaches to Scripture.*[62] Professor Greer admits in a candid forward that he is not personally sympathetic to classical Anglicanism and his book makes it plain that he is firmly opposed to Evangelicalism, especially its doctrine of the 'verbal inerrancy' of Scripture. But in spite of his personal views on the subject, he has been forced by his research to come to the conclusion that Anglicanism in its formative years was a Reformed church, fully committed to *sola Scriptura* and following a doctrine so close to 'verbal inerrancy' as to be virtually indistinguishable from it. Moreover, he demonstrates quite clearly that Richard Hooker also belonged to that tradition and cannot legitimately be regarded as the author of the three-fold doctrine of authority that circulates

---

[61] This has even been true of Roman Catholics. The Douai Bible, which was produced shortly before the Authorized Version of 1611 was extensively revised in the eighteenth century – mainly by admitting a generous dose of the AV into it!
[62] (New York: Crossroad, 2006).

under his name. In spite of himself, Professor Greer is forced to place Anglicanism in the mainstream of Reformed Protestantism from which it did not deviate until the rise of Tractarianism in the nineteenth century.[63]

Classical Anglicanism held that 'the Bible alone is the religion of Protestants' and interpreted the sacred text along the lines of the covenant theology developed by the followers of John Calvin.[64] It developed a number of different streams of thought within this broader paradigm, but it has remained a coherently Reformed tradition. This fact is being increasingly emphasised by historians, who are making it clearer than it has been for a long time that the rise of Anglo-Catholicism was an aberration which has seriously distorted modern perceptions of the nature of Anglicanism.[65]

Of course, as Anglo-Catholics have long wanted to insist, the Anglican Communion is but one small part of the universal church and has always recognized this. Article 34 expressly states that it is not necessary for traditions and ceremonies to be the same everywhere and accepts that real diversity can and does exist in the Christian world. The only criterion by which local customs and usages must be measured is the Word of God, by which the Reformers meant Holy Scripture. For that reason, Anglicans welcome Christians of every tradition to share the Lord's Supper with us as long as they are baptised and communicant members of their own church. This is practical ecumenical hospitality and a clear recognition that it is not necessary for someone to be an Anglican in order for us to accept him as a fellow Christian. Church membership is more demanding than this, of course, but not excessively so. All that is required is Trinitarian baptism, a

---

[63] Professor Greer is not himself a Tractarian but a follower of Samuel Taylor Coleridge who was their contemporary but whose vision of the Bible and theology was rather different from theirs.

[64] The phrase is attributed to William Chillingworth (1602-44) who happened to be the godson of Archbishop Laud!

[65] See for example P. B. Nockles, *The Oxford Movement in context: Anglican high churchmanship 1760-1857* (Cambridge: CUP, 1997) and F. M. Turner, *John Henry Newman* (New Haven: Yale University Press, 2002).

profession of faith and confirmation by the bishop, though membership may be extended to people who desire confirmation in the expectation that they will be confirmed as soon as is practically possible.[66]

The distinctive teachings of Anglicanism do not really impinge on most ordinary people unless and until they seek to become ordained ministers. The clergy are the teachers and public representatives of the church and it is only right that a higher degree of understanding and commitment should be required of them. It would not be too much to say that it is the widespread failure to maintain these standards that is a major cause of the current crisis in the Anglican Communion. Far too many people have been ordained without adequate training and many of them have only a vague knowledge of what the church's official teaching is. In England for example, it is virtually certain that the majority of ordained clergy today have never studied the Thirty-nine Articles of Religion (to which they have formally assented) and thanks to recent liturgical revisions, many are now unfamiliar with the Book of Common Prayer. They may have studied it in a course on liturgy, but they have seldom used it in public worship and have not made it central to their private devotional lives.[67] As for the Homilies, it is a rare clergyman indeed who has read them, or even seen a copy! No wonder there is such confusion about the true meaning of Anglicanism, when its charter documents are unstudied and virtually unknown to those whose duty it is to teach them and uphold the doctrine they contain.

It is true of course that the Thirty-nine Articles of Religion and the Homilies which expound their teaching were products of their time and reflect the concerns of the sixteenth century. They had already undergone one revision before they were approved in February 1563 and again (in their present form) in April 1571, and

---

[66] This is not much of a problem today, but there have been some curious situations in the past. In the American colonies, for example, there were no bishops and so hardly any of the Anglicans there had been confirmed, though they were clearly accepted as church members!

[67] Ordained clergy are required to say Morning and Evening Prayer daily, but how many actually do? And of those, how many use the 1662 BCP?

probably they were never intended to remain as they were indefinitely.[68] In some respects they could do with further revision, as was already recognized by Archbishop John Whitgift (1583-1604), Archbishop James Ussher (1581-1656) and the men of the Westminster Assembly (1643-7), most of whom were Anglicans. It is largely for political reasons that the Lambeth Articles of 1595 (composed by Whitgift), the Irish Articles of 1615 (defended, if not actually composed by Ussher) and the Westminster Confession of 1646 are not regarded as part of the Anglican theological inheritance today, though of course Anglicans who honour their Reformed heritage are happy to accept them. Nevertheless, the Thirty-nine Articles represent a balanced and nuanced approach to questions of Christian doctrine and in that respect they remain a guideline for us today. They state what needs to be affirmed and reject what must be denied, without advancing dubious or secondary propositions. They are clearly opposed to the exaggerated claims of Rome, but do not deny its status as a Christian church and do not call the pope the Antichrist. At a time when the Council of Trent was busily excommunicating anyone who disagreed with it, this was a remarkable act of forbearance and discretion – an ecumenical act in a most unecumenical age.[69] The Homilies are best understood as a commentary on the Articles, but the fact that they were intended as sermons means that they have retained a vitality which more abstract tomes of theology lack, and it is surprising how accessible to modern audiences they can be. Like the Articles, they address the questions of the sixteenth century and sometimes need to be updated, but the extent to which they have survived the test of time is truly remarkable. They ought to be recovered, if not by ordinary congregations, then certainly by those seeking to minister to them, who can be encouraged to adapt their teaching for modern use.

Finally, we have the Book of Common Prayer, another text

---

[68] This was 1562 in the old calendar (which began the new year on 25 March), and this is why that date sometimes appears in connection with them.

[69] It might be added that Queen Elizabeth initially withheld assent to Article 29, for fear of offending the Lutherans. It was not finally accepted until 1571 when the Articles assumed their present form.

which underwent substantial revision before reaching its classical form in 1662, but which still reflects its original purpose of providing the church with a biblical form of worship to convey the gospel message in a way that is accessible to the average worshipper. It is in the BCP that key doctrines like justification by faith alone and penal substitutionary atonement receive their fullest expression, not as abstract propositions but as re-enacted realities. Those who participate in Holy Communion according to the 1662 rite are committing themselves in an existential way to these timeless truths at the heart of the gospel. Here is the true glory of Anglicanism, a church in which the gospel is proclaimed by the liturgy even when the preacher or celebrant does not fully grasp it himself, and a community in which every believer can meet with God in worship regardless of what others may think, say or do, without falling into subjectivism or idiosyncrasy. This is our heritage and this is what we have to offer to the Christian world – mere, basic Christianity expressed in clear, objective and compelling tones.

3. Heresy

3.1. The origin of the concept

In Christian theology, a heresy is any belief that deviates from the orthodox norm. The Greek word *haeresis* is found in pre-Christian literature and derives from the verb meaning 'take' or 'choose'. In the time of Jesus it could still be used in its literal sense, but it had already come to be the term to describe philosophical schools in the pagan world and spiritual traditions among the Jews. In the New Testament it covers both the Pharisees and the Sadducees, especially in the Acts of the Apostles.[70] It also occurs three times in Acts with reference to Christianity, though the early Christians never regarded their faith merely as one form of Judaism among others.[71] For them, the gospel of Christ was the fulfilment of the law and the prophets, a new beginning for God's people who would henceforth include Gentiles as well as Jews. A Pharisee or a Sadducee who became a Christian had to abandon his previous identity because the religious context in which that identity had some meaning had ceased to exist. There was no carry-over of Jewish *haereses* into the Christian church, although there were Judaizing tendencies in the first generation which reflect Pharisaic influence more than anything else.

The tendency to develop a sectarian mentality is present in every school of thought and so it was only natural for Pharisees, Sadducees, Essenes and others to suppose that their interpretation of the Mosaic law was the correct one, and insist that others were not fully Jewish. But in spite of these rivalries, they seem to have lived side by side with a degree of mutual tolerance that they did not extend to Samaritans or Christians.

Within the church, the Apostle Paul apparently regarded the existence of different schools of thought as a necessary

---

[70] Acts 5:17; 15:5; 26:5.
[71] Acts 24:5,14; 28:22.

development, not because Christianity lacked content but because without them the truth would not be discerned as clearly as it should be.[72] We can easily understand this from our own experience in other areas, where discussion and debate often help to clarify issues that would otherwise remain dormant or unexplored. However, it is clear from the New Testament that tolerance of different opinions did not extend to false teaching, which was strongly resisted. The Apostle Paul's correspondence is often directed against it, although we cannot be entirely sure what it was. Judaizing tendencies were certainly part of it, and had to be combatted, but whether they would count as 'heresies' in the classical sense is doubtful.[73] In Paul's mind, to continue to practise Jewish laws and customs was harmless for Jewish Christians, but to try to impose them on Gentile converts was to give them a status to which they were not entitled and (in effect) to invalidate the gospel. Circumcision was an obvious case in point. For Jews this signified belonging to the ancient covenant people of God, and in that sense Paul had no quarrel with it. He even had Timothy circumcised when the latter was about to embark on his missionary career, because he did not want to cause needless offence to Jews, who would not have listened to anyone claiming to be Jewish if he was not circumcised.[74] But Paul's willingness to become 'a Jew to the Jews' was a matter of flexibility on secondary matters, and not an essential principle of the Christian faith.[75] When others suggested that circumcision was essential, he reacted strongly against them and pointed out that their view compromised the efficacy of Christ's saving work, which is the very heart of the gospel.[76] What at one level was a difference of opinion and practice,

---

[72] 1 Corinthians 11:19.

[73] See Galatians 2:15-21 and the entire argument of that epistle.

[74] Acts 16:1-3. Timothy was the child of a mixed marriage, but his mother was Jewish, and so he was counted as such in Jewish law. It is possible that he was not circumcised at birth because his Gentile father would not allow it. Many centuries later, we find that Augustine of Hippo was the child of a pagan father and a Christian mother, but was not baptised – evidently for the same reason. It is still the custom in mixed marriages around the Mediterranean for the children (especially the boys) to be brought up in the father's religion, not the mother's.

[75] See 1 Corinthians 9:20.

[76] Galatians 2:21.

something 'indifferent' as we might now say, had been interpreted in a way that made it fundamental and therefore unacceptable. In those circumstances Paul rejected the need for circumcision and insisted that all the Apostles, including those like Peter who ministered mainly to Jews, should agree with him about this.[77]

The New Testament demonstrates that on a matter of fundamental doctrine no dissent could be tolerated inside the church. Paul told the Galatians that anyone who preached a different gospel was to be declared 'anathema' and this intolerance is typical of the Apostles generally.[78] It is hard to say to what extent the Apostles were faced with the sort of doctrinal deviations which gave rise to later heresies, although there is some evidence to suggest that they were and that they could use the word 'heresy' to describe them.[79] Be that as it may, there can be no doubt that heresies as we understand them appeared in the second century and were dangerous enough to attract opposition from the church authorities. Irenaeus (d. c. 200) was the first major Christian writer to tackle the problem head-on in *The detection and refutation of the so-called 'knowledge'*, a work more usually known today as *Against all heresies*, which is invaluable for the detailed analysis it gives of deviant forms of Christianity that are now lumped together as 'gnosticism'.[80] In the course of doing this Irenaeus was forced to explain what the true Christian teaching was, and so by default he became the church's first systematic theologian. Irenaeus was

---

[77] Galatians 2:1-14.

[78] Galatians 1:8. See also 2 Peter 2:1, 1 John 2:18-19, 2 John 7, Jude 4.

[79] See for example, 2 Peter 2:1.

[80] From the Greek word *gnosis*, meaning 'knowledge'. The term was invented in the early nineteenth century and has an esoteric flavour to it which is lacking in Irenaeus, whose aim was not to refute *gnosis* as such but to replace false knowledge by true. Some people continue to believe that Irenaeus was a minority voice who somehow managed to impose his views on a pluralistic church, thereby creating both 'orthodoxy' and 'heresy'. This opinion was developed by Walter Bauer (1877-1960), whose book *Rechtgläubigkeit und Ketzerei im ältesten Christentum* was published in 1934 and translated into English in 1972 as *orthodoxy and heresy in earliest Christianity* (London: SCM). Bauer's thesis has been refuted many times and is not really tenable, but it continues to influence the thought of people like Elaine Pagels and Bart Ehrman. For a recent evaluation of this see Bock, *Missing Gospels*.

followed by Tertullian (fl. c. 196-212) who performed much the same task for the Latin-speaking world. They appear to have been successful, because the danger of 'gnosticism' gradually receded. By the time Christianity became a legal religion in 313 it was no longer a serious threat, but other problems had arisen to take its place. Arianism was the most serious of these and it was to be many centuries before the church finally managed to extinguish it. Shortly after that happened, Isidore of Seville (c. 600) made a list of the different heresies known to him. This list was later incorporated by Pope Gregory IX into his *Liber extra* (1234), which made it the classical definition of heresy in the canon law of the medieval church.

3.2.   Heresy as a capital crime

By that time new deviations had arisen, most notably the revived form of Manichaeism associated with the so-called Cathars of Albi and other parts of what is now southern France.[81] The classical heresies mentioned by Isidore had ceased to exist as such, and the church's apparent inability to repress contemporary heresies increased fear of them among the people. This led to demands that heretics should be put to death so as to prevent their plague from spreading. Execution was to be by burning at the stake, a form chosen partly for secular and partly for 'spiritual' reasons. In the secular world, a nobleman had the right to be beheaded whereas a peasant would be hanged, but heresy transcended social class and so a neutral form of execution had to be devised. It was also claimed that fire was a purifying element which would burn the evil out of a penitent heretic's soul, making it possible for him (or more rarely, her) to be saved.[82]

---

[81] They were closely related to the Bogomils of Bulgaria and are called by various names even today. Their principal doctrinal tenet was dualism, the belief that good and evil were equal, opposing forces, which led to the conclusion that those on the side of good had to be perfect, since no form of evil could exist in a world governed by the power of good. The Albigensians were defeated and virtually exterminated in a crusade led by the French king Philip Augustus in 1215.

[82] See 1 Corinthians 3:11-15.

It was fairly easy to condemn the dualistic Cathars because they rejected the sovereignty of God over creation, a doctrine which was clearly affirmed in the Bible and in the creeds of the church. But there were other people who held questionable beliefs and who were a nuisance to the authorities, although they did not deny the classical credal tenets of the faith. John Wycliffe was a case in point. He challenged the church of his day and dissented from its teachings about papal authority and transubstantiation, but was that enough to make him a heretic? The appearance of universities from the thirteenth century onwards had created a class of people who were skilled in theological debate, which would not have taken place if a certain latitude of opinion had not been tolerated, at least in academic circles. It is possible to see Wycliffe's condemnation for 'heresy' as essentially a form of scholarly in-fighting, in which his opponents were stronger than he was and got to the church authorities, including the pope, before he did. Wycliffe was forced to leave Oxford in 1382 but he managed to die in his bed two years later, because at that time England had not legislated against heresy or provided any punishment for it.

One of the reasons for this was that heresy could only be judged by the church authorities, and they insisted on capital punishment for those who were convicted. It was generally regarded as a biblical principle that officers of the church could not put anyone to death themselves, because they could not sully their hands with blood. All they could do was pass a sentence of condemnation and turn the guilty party over to the state for punishment. The biblical precedent cited for this was the case of Jesus, who had been tried and condemned by the Jewish Sanhedrin for blasphemy, but who could only be put to death by the state authorities.[83] Ironically though, medieval authorities often turned out to be uncannily like Pontius Pilate – ignorant of the issues, inclined to pronounce the 'heretic' innocent of any crime and highly reluctant to execute the sentence against him. It went against the grain for kings to defer to the wishes of the clergy, who operated under a separate legal system and had a different set of

---

[83] Luke 23:1-25.

priorities. Wycliffe may have been an irritation to some prominent churchmen, but he had powerful lay supporters, not least because he disputed the pope's right to levy taxes on the English people, and he would probably have escaped execution even if there had been a heresy law in place at that time.

Heresy was not made a capital crime in England until 1401, following a *coup d'état* in which Henry IV had deposed his cousin Richard II with the help of some prominent churchmen. In return for their support, Henry IV bowed to their wishes concerning heresy, but although the law was on the statute books, enforcing it was another matter. English executioners had no experience of burning people at the stake and were reluctant to undertake what they regarded as a barbarous form of punishment. There was also the problem of defining what heresy was, and few people were prepared to trust a church hierarchy whose motives in condemning men like Wycliffe were mixed, to say the least. Nevertheless, a synod of the clergy was held at Oxford in 1407 and approved a list of heresies, among which were such things as preaching without a licence and translating the Bible into English – measures which were clearly designed to counter the Lollards, as Wycliffe's followers were called. For the next twenty-five years or so there was a series of heresy trials, aimed mainly at trying to stamp out Lollardy and attacking the Franciscan order in particular, which was thought to be a seedbed of it. A look at the records shows that the church had little trouble getting away with this in the reign of Henry V (1413-22) who spent most of his time campaigning in France and needed the church's support for his wars, or during the minority of Henry VI (1422-37).[84] But there was a marked falling off in the number of heresy trials after that, and by the time of the Reformation they had become very rare.

The nature of the English reformation was such that it was difficult to distinguish heresy from treason against the king, and in 1534 the heresy statute was replaced to take account of the new

---

[84] Henry VI became king at the age of nine months and reached his majority in 1437. He ruled until 1461, when he was deposed, though he made a brief comeback in 1470-1, after which he was put to death.

circumstances. Henry VIII put some people to death for denying Catholic doctrine (in particular, transubstantiation) and under Mary I (1553-8) over 200 people were burnt at the stake. Almost all of these were Protestants, whose 'heresy' was that they rejected the authority of the Roman church. The heresy statute was finally repealed in 1677, though by that time it had fallen into disuse. After 1558 it was employed mainly to fight against witchcraft, and the last person to be burnt in England was put to death in 1612 for indulging in occult practices.

It is important to realise that the heresy statute did not fade away because religious dissent disappeared. On the contrary, it was because dissent took so many forms and affected such a large number of people that taking legal proceedings against them as 'heretics' became virtually impossible. There were periodic crackdowns against sectarians and Roman Catholics, but these were political in nature and seldom ventured into the theological realm. For example, when the pope excommunicated Queen Elizabeth I in 1570 and advised her subjects to work for her overthrow, she had no choice but to retaliate. This produced a number of Catholic 'martyrs' in both England and Ireland, who are still celebrated as such by the Roman Catholic Church. However, these Catholics were not prosecuted as 'heretics' but as traitors, as can be seen from the fact that they were beheaded or hanged, not burnt at the stake.

3.3. Heresy trials in modern times

The disappearance of heresy from the statute books in 1677 did not put an end to it, but it did create a more delicate situation for the church. Non-conformists and Roman Catholic recusants suffered some discrimination because of their beliefs but they were seldom put to death for them.[85] There was however a certain tendency for

---

[85] A tragic exception to this was the execution of Oliver Plunkett, Catholic archbishop of Armagh, on 1 July 1681. Plunkett was caught up in the hysteria surrounding the so-called 'Popish plot', a fictitious conspiracy which was supposedly trying to undo the Protestant reformation. Inexcusable though Plunkett's murder was, its exceptional character proves the general rule.

heresy to proliferate among dissenters, and in the early eighteenth century almost all the English Presbyterians became Unitarians. Apologists for the establishment saw this as a natural consequence of dissent and lambasted it accordingly, but there was nothing they could do about it. A more serious source of danger for the church came from people claiming to be its members who were disseminating ideas incompatible with the Christian faith. This had begun in the 1640s under the patronage of Lord Falkland and his Great Tew circle,[86] but at that time the general breakdown of civil and ecclesiastical government had made prosecuting them impossible. After the restoration in 1660, the public expression of heterodox ideas was politically unwise, and most of those who held them kept quiet, but in 1695 the licensing act, which had provided for the censorship of religious publications, was allowed to lapse and freedom of the press became a reality. The result was a spate of books and pamphlets denouncing the established church, some of which went so far as to question the underpinnings of Christianity itself. In the early eighteenth century, the convocations of Canterbury and Ireland condemned a few books which they regarded as particularly outrageous, but the government was unwilling to prosecute the offenders. The only consolation the church obtained was the blasphemy act of 1698, which forbade anyone to insult the Christian religion in an outrageous manner.

That statute is still in force and it was successfully invoked as recently as 1977, when the late Mary Whitehouse prosecuted a homosexual publication for daring to treat Jesus and his disciples as homosexuals. Recently there has been some questioning of the continuing relevance of this law, but as opinion is divided between those who want to abolish it and those who want to extend it to cover other religions as well, nothing has happened so far, though following a recent vote in the House of Lords to repeal it, it will probably disappear before long. The blasphemy law may have curbed excesses, but it could not prevent attacks on the Christian religion which became more frequent as time went on. Inevitably, many people in the church thought that the government of the day

---

[86] Great Tew was the name of his country estate. One of his followers was Christopher Herbert, elder brother of the poet George Herbert.

was responsible for this, and because the state appointed the bishops, they came under suspicion of complicity with its 'godless' policies. A known supporter of those policies was Benjamin Hoadly, who became an object of attack as soon as he was made bishop of Bangor in 1716. On 31 March 1717 Hoadly preached a sermon before King George I in which he claimed that because the kingdom of God was not of this world, the visible Church of England could not be regarded as the only true church and dissent from it should therefore be tolerated.[87] Many in the church were outraged at this and demanded that he be put on trial for heresy, but before this could be done the Canterbury convocation was prorogued and did not meet again for the transaction of business until 5 November 1852. Hoadly, however, went from strength to strength and ended his days as bishop of Winchester, much to the disgust of conservatives within the church. But even if they had succeeded in bringing him to trial, it is hard to see that they could have won their case, since what Hoadly said was scarcely heretical. As was to happen many times in the future, the conservatives had misjudged the situation, overplayed their hand and lost out to the liberals of the day. Hoadly was far from being the most extreme of these, but by causing the machinery of prosecution to be silenced, the conservative element in the church inadvertently opened the door for much more radical people to express their views with impunity.

By the time the convocations were revived in the mid-nineteenth century, the Church of England had lost its religious monopoly and could no longer hope to invoke the aid of the state in defence of its doctrine. Furthermore, a decision of Lord Hardwicke in 1736 had established the principle that the church courts could not exercise canonical jurisdiction over the laity, which made it virtually impossible to prosecute anyone for heresy who was not in

---

[87] Like William III before him, George I was a member of the Reformed church and not an Anglican, though (unlike William III) he was obliged to conform to the Church of England by virtue of the Act of Succession (1701). It is not clear whether he agreed with Hoadly's sermon or not; as his English was very poor, he probably did not understand a word of it! On the Bangorian controversy, as it is called, see A. Starkie, *The Church of England and the Bangorian controversy, 1716-1721* (Woodbridge, 2007).

holy orders.[88] Some people believed that the revival of the convocations would lead to renewed heresy-hunting, and there was evidence to justify this fear. At that time the Church of England was starting to divide into Anglo-Catholic, Evangelical and 'broad' camps, and there was a real danger that one of them would use whatever means it had at its disposal to attack the others. The bishop of Exeter had already prosecuted Charles Gorham (1787-1857) for denying baptismal regeneration, which he claimed was the official teaching of the church. The bishop's views were upheld in the Court of Arches in 1849 but that judgment was overturned by the Judicial Committee of the Privy Council a year later. Some Anglo-Catholics left for Rome in protest at this, but had the bishop won his case he would have driven the Evangelicals out of the Church of England. The issue was clearly one that divided the church along party lines and it was still fresh in the memory a decade later, when the Canterbury convocation condemned *Essays and reviews*, a symposium by some liberal churchmen of the time (21 June 1861). Two years later, the guns were turned on Bishop Colenso of Natal, who had denied the literal truth of the Bible, and in 1864 there was a further condemnation of *Essays and reviews*, although nothing could be done to punish the accused because the church lacked any effective form of sanction. A further attempt was made in 1891 to condemn Charles Gore's *Lux mundi*, but it was warded off before it could reach the floor of the convocation, and after that official attempts to censure views deemed to be heretical ceased altogether.

The reasons for the cessation of heresy trials in the late nineteenth century are complex and have to do both with internal church affairs and the impact of the outside world. Inside the church, the eighteenth century had been a time of relative calm. Bishops generally came from the upper echelons of society and they often appointed their own family members to the most

---

[88] The 1736 decision actually said that the canons of the church did not apply to lay people unless they had been ratified by parliament (which the 1604 canons never were). These need not have been a serious impediment to the prosecution of the laity but the ruling was interpreted very broadly and convinced most people that it amounted to a general prohibition.

desirable church positions. In the countryside, local squires often did the same, putting younger sons or nephews into parishes and generally making sure that nothing disturbed the rhythm of agricultural life. But as England industrialised, this rural church was put under enormous strain. City parishes were overwhelmed and could not minister effectively to the thousands of new inhabitants who suddenly turned up on their doorstep. Meanwhile, the Evangelical revival was making inroads among the lower classes of society, who had never been closely connected to church life, and by 1800 they were organised up and down the country, often as semi-independent congregations. Evangelicals eventually began to get parish appointments, but this was a slow process and did not occur fast enough to prevent the wholesale defection of the Methodists in the early nineteenth century. The rise of Evangelicalism created a situation in which the boundaries between the establishment and dissent were blurred,[89] and the abolition of most of the restrictions on non-Anglicans in 1828-9 created a large non-conformist electorate which wanted root-and-branch reform of both church and society.

One response to this was the rise of Tractarianism, later to become Anglo-Catholicism. Unlike the Evangelicals, who were not very interested in church structures, the Anglo-Catholics laid great emphasis on them – in theory. In practice however, they undermined the establishment by trying to introduce ritual practices and unfamiliar usages which had disappeared at the Reformation.[90] The legality of this was questioned by many, and there were numerous court cases directed against ritualists, in the course of which some clergymen were actually sent to prison. This created martyrs to the cause and discredited the 'persecutors', as they were seen in the eyes of the wider public, which thought that such behaviour was un-Christian. Evangelicals were caught up in

---

[89] They still are for Evangelicals, who usually prefer to work with those who share their spiritual outlook rather than with other Anglicans who do not.

[90] With some practices like auricular confession to a priest, it is hard to say why they disappeared and the Prayer Book continued to make residual provision for them. However, there was no doubt that they had vanished, whether by official condemnation of them or not.

these legal battles and their reputation suffered as a result, even if they often won their cases in the courts. It was an unenviable situation for them to find themselves in, having to defend the Protestant character of the church against a form of internal dissent which thought nothing of breaking the rules, in spite of its supposedly 'high' ecclesiology. Many of the bishops did what they could to suppress ritualism, but their hands were often tied by the rights of beneficed incumbents and the refusal of many of them to obey their theoretically revered 'father-in-God'. By the end of the nineteenth century many people had grown weary of court battles over ritual matters, which were usually conducted in a spirit devoid of Christian charity, and were relieved when the Clergy Discipline Act of 1892 took cases of this kind out of the public arena.

3.4. The doctrinal paralysis of the modern church

As Anglo-Catholics and Evangelicals battled it out in the courts, a very different spirit was making headway in the country at large and in the church. This was nineteenth-century liberalism, which was characterised by a sometimes naively optimistic belief in science, progress and rational enquiry generally. Churchgoing was still fashionable and public figures were expected to profess some form of Christianity, but there was a spirit of tolerance abroad which refused to define this too closely. The growth of historical inquiry led to a widespread questioning of the Bible, which was reinforced by the emergence of Darwinian theories of evolution. The church could not remain immune from these developments, although for a long time the majority did its best to suppress theological liberalism, which was always much less popular at grass roots level than it was in the universities. The end result was a church in which a wide range of practice was tolerated and contradictory views on any number of subjects were allowed to co-exist in peace, if not in harmony. Though the original disputes had been mainly about ritual and ceremonial matters, by 1900 more serious doctrinal questions were being debated as well. Many Evangelicals were adopting a more liberal approach to Scripture and abandoning belief in things like eternal punishment in hell and penal substitutionary atonement, regarding them as cruel and barbaric doctrines unworthy of a God of love. Some Anglo-

Catholics were also abandoning traditional doctrines by taking refuge in the concept of 'metaphor' and by placing greater stress on liturgy than on the beliefs underlying it. By the 1920s the Evangelicals had split into two opposing camps. The Catholic wing of the church did not divide so easily, but as many of their ritualistic practices were increasingly adopted by the broad middle ground of the church, it became easier for the liberals among them to present an appearance of orthodoxy while harbouring liberal and even radical ideas at variance with traditional Christianity.[91]

During this period, the formularies of the church[92] were increasingly disregarded by everyone except the conservative Evangelicals. The canons of the church, passed in 1604 and virtually unrevised since then, were ignored and sometimes ridiculed for their obvious anachronisms. Church discipline became almost impossible to exercise and those inclined to insist on it were regarded as extremists out of touch with the feeling of the church as a whole. In the 1960s a fresh wave of reforming zeal took over, and huge changes were put into effect. The canons were revised (1964-9), a new General Synod with legislative powers was created (1970) and liturgical revision was begun in earnest. By 2000 the traditional formularies had been effectively relegated to the sidelines, though they were not abolished. The form and conduct of public worship had lost any sense of uniformity and theology was at even more of a discount than it had been before the great changes began. Observers both inside and outside the church were remarking on the low standard of debate in General Synod, especially when a doctrinal question was raised for discussion, and the competence of the church's main legislative organ to decide anything at all became a matter of serious doubt in many quarters – with good reason. Untrained, part-time and forced to consider a range of issues beyond the grasp of non-specialists, the members of General Synod were left floundering, and open to manipulation

---

[91] It is interesting to observe that a similar pattern developed in the Roman Catholic Church, where it became obvious after the Second Vatican Council (1962-5).
[92] The Thirty-nine Articles of Religion, the Book of Common Prayer, the Ordinal and the Homilies.

by pressure groups of different kinds. The result is that General Synod is now incapable of making the kinds of judgments which might be expected of such a body and is all too easily swayed by the rhetoric of a few dedicated campaigners.[93]

In the wider church, chaos reigns. There is no control of any kind exercised over the laity, nor is it easy to see how there could be any if the lay person in question is not a church employee. A clergyman may be disciplined for refusing to baptize the babies of non-attending parishioners, but not for having a sex-change operation. Beliefs are more than ever a matter of individual choice. It is not always realised how recent this loss of theological discipline has been and how swiftly it occurred. When the late John Robinson, bishop of Woolwich, published *Honest to God* in 1963, in which he questioned many traditional Christian doctrines, he was rusticated to Trinity College, Cambridge, although no further action was taken. But in 1984 the archbishop of York snubbed more than 13,000 protesters and consecrated David Jenkins as bishop of Durham, even though Jenkins had not only denied the doctrine of the bodily resurrection of Christ but had publicly ridiculed it. York Minster was struck by lightning shortly afterwards, a strange coincidence which was noticed by many, but apart from that, there was no reaction. When the 1998 Lambeth Conference issued a declaration against homosexual practice that was approved by the overwhelming number of bishops present, no fewer than forty-six English diocesans and suffragans announced that they would pay no attention to it, and nothing was said or done to rebuke them. By no means all of the bishops agreed with this behaviour of course, but it is a rare prelate who will stand up and be counted, as the recent debates over homosexuality have shown. Here, as so often in the past, the liberals make the running in public while others keep their mouths shut so as not to destroy the appearance of 'collegiality'. There are supposed to be upwards of

---

[93] It is never easy to combine expertise with democracy. The synods of the early church did not try to do that – they were restricted to bishops who were expected to know what they were talking about. Whether a similar restriction in the modern Church of England would produce the same result may be doubted, even if it were possible.

thirty Evangelicals in the house of bishops at the present time, but sadly few of them can be relied on to stand for a consistently orthodox theological position. The others come and go and seldom stick their heads above the parapet on any controversial issue.

3.5. *Dealing with heresy today*

In a climate like this one, trying to discipline heresy is bound to be problematic. There can be no doubt that it still exists, but the current climate of opinion is such that it is impossible to do anything about it. Legal proceedings against alleged heretics are theoretically possible but for several reasons they would not work. The enormous cost is one obvious deterrent, as is the fact that the secular media would invariably side with the accused against what they would perceive (rightly or wrongly) as an 'intolerant' minority in the church. Besides that, no-one could guarantee that the judges appointed to try the case would be committed to upholding orthodox beliefs, and some of them might not even be aware that such a thing as 'orthodoxy' exists. It is all too easy to imagine a trial being held before a liberal bishop who might easily be more culpable than the defendant and inclined to use the occasion to denounce the official teaching of the church in the name of 'freedom' – or even of 'love'. An accused person could also appeal to a different hermeneutic of Scripture and/or tradition of the church, and might well escape censure on that basis. If David Jenkins had been put on trial, he would probably have claimed that he believed in a 'spiritual resurrection' (whatever that might be) and that he therefore stood within the bounds of traditional Christianity, even though most observers (and all traditionalists) would disagree with him. Such verbal sleight of hand has often been used as a way of 'reinterpreting' the church's official doctrinal statements, and in this respect the Anglican tradition of comprehensiveness does not work in favour of the orthodox.

But even if a miracle occurred and the accused party in such a case were to be found guilty, what sanctions could be imposed? It is extremely difficult to imagine anything that would achieve its object. If a bishop were to withdraw a clergyman's preaching licence, it is all but certain that a more sympathetic diocesan elsewhere would grant him one, and his punishment would consist of nothing more than having to move from one diocese to another. In 1994 Anthony Freeman, a priest in the diocese of Chichester, had his license revoked because he had ceased to believe in God. Sympathy for him was immediately expressed in both Oxford and Worcester (his previous diocese), and although he has not held a clerical appointment since that time, he is still listed in *Crockford's Clerical Directory* as a priest of the Church of England! It is hard to think of a more obvious example of heresy than this, but if even it cannot be satisfactorily resolved, what hope is there for less extreme cases?

A further factor which has to be taken into consideration is that there is an element in the church which is prepared to persecute orthodox believers and drive them out of the church altogether. Measures designed to root out heretics could be turned against traditionalists, especially if the compulsory acceptance of recent innovations like the ordination of women came to be used as the yardstick of 'orthodoxy'. So far this has not happened in the Church of England, but a glance around the Anglican Communion shows just how worrying a prospect it is. There the issues which have been chosen to define the new Anglicanism are two – the ordination of women and the admission of practising homosexuals at all levels of the church's ministry. Dissent on the former point is now a matter for discipline in both the USA and Canada, and in the USA one or two rectors have been removed from their posts for disputing the latter, though that has not yet become official policy across the board. Neither of these is a doctrinal question in itself, but both have serious doctrinal implications. As with the gnosticism of the early church, they touch on the doctrine of creation and for that reason they are matters of primary importance for our faith. The view that whatever difference there is between men and women has been overcome by the death of Christ is based on a misunderstanding of Galatians 3:28 and is clearly contradicted by other parts of the New Testament.[94] But such is the power of political correctness that these objections (not to mention the universal tradition of the church since apostolic times) have simply

---

[94] 1 Corinthians 11:2-16; 1 Timothy 2:11-15.

been ignored, and in some Anglican churches it is now practically impossible for anyone who openly dissents from the liberal consensus to be ordained. The inability of so many church leaders to understand that this is a problem is eclipsed only by the widespread conviction among them that orthodox believers are bent on practising a form of discrimination against women which ought to be as unlawful in the church as it is in the state. The homosexual question is a natural outgrowth of this, because once the gender barrier is dismissed as irrelevant, why should it matter what a person's sexual orientation is? Of course, nobody has ever suggested that people with homosexual inclinations ought to be excluded from the ministry; what is at issue is homosexual practice, which is condemned in Scripture as unnatural.[95] Once again, every hermeneutical trick is produced by homosexual activists in order to get around this clear teaching of the Apostle Paul and the whole question dissolves into an emotionally-charged wrangle about 'justice' and 'rights' for the supposedly 'oppressed'. As usual, the orthodox are portrayed as unloving and dogmatic, whereas those who want change are presented as sympathetic people in tune with the spirit of the times.

For all these reasons, it can be safely concluded that no appeal to the formularies or judicial organs of the Church of England in a matter of heresy is likely to succeed, and that anyone who tried such a thing would be blackballed and effectively driven out of the church, either by those of a different persuasion or by those who do not want to rock the boat. Furthermore, this repression of the orthodox would most likely be regarded as an act of 'justice', since anyone accused of heresy would be portrayed as a victim of intolerance. It is a depressing scenario for those who care about the church's life and teaching in the sight of God and who believe that one day we shall face a judgment higher than that of any secular tribunal if we fail to defend the faith once delivered to the saints. For the time being, it seems that heresy is here to stay, and that any strategy aimed at dealing with it will have to think in new ways if it is to have any hope of success.

---

[95] Romans 1:27.

The only way that heresy can be refuted in the modern world is by argument, and the only way it will be defeated is by changing the climate of opinion generally. The theologically decadent atmosphere in which we now live did not come into being overnight; it emerged from several centuries of argument and debate, which was initiated by radical thinkers who suffered for their temerity at the time. They eventually succeeded because their views were essentially no more than adaptations of opinions that were already circulating widely in the secular sphere. The theologians of the 1960s who proclaimed that 'our vision of God must go' understood this perfectly well; it was one of their main arguments that the church had lost its voice in the world because it had failed to keep pace with modern thought. Those of us who disagree with this assessment have to accept that we are on the defensive, even if we are a majority in parts of the church. Christians have always belonged to a counter-culture, even when the church has played a dominant part in society. Earlier generations had to struggle against the worldliness of church leaders, many of whom put politics and profit well ahead of prophecy. Today we are less involved in secular pursuits than our forbears were, but that is mainly because the church has been marginalised in a society which thinks it can do without religion. Our battle is one which concerns the fundamental question of 'world view'. We have to argue not only for the existence of supernatural truth, but for the legitimacy of its primacy in our lives. The world we live in has shut out God, and regards his followers as fanatics who are a potential danger to peace, order and good government. It sees no essential difference between Islamic terrorism and Evangelical Christianity, because in its eyes both are equally irrational and unwelcome. In this climate, a debate about the divinity of Christ is an absurdity, and the notion that someone should be disciplined for not subscribing to a fairy-tale is literally beyond belief. As Christians, we may find this painful to accept, since for so long the culture we live in paid at least lip-service to our values and understanding of reality. That is no longer true, and the beliefs which once made heresy and its repression a central social duty no longer command the same general assent. Intellectually speaking, we have returned to the catacombs of ancient Rome and become once more an underground movement. In the longer scheme of things we shall one day resurface and reclaim our inheritance, but no-one can say when that day will come. All we know for sure is that we are called to take up our cross and follow Jesus, knowing only that we must be prepared to suffer for him if we have any hope of reigning with him in glory.[96]

There is no easy answer or magic formula which can bring this change about. The warfare we wage is spiritual and our victory is in the hand of God, not in any clever schemes we might devise. Our chief weapons in the struggle remain what they have always been – prayer and obedience. When Jesus faced his final agony on earth, he went into the garden to pray, and when he prayed he said: 'Not my will, but your will be done.'[97] As servants we are not greater than our Master, and only when we learn to walk in his footsteps shall we see the victory of his kingdom in our lives. This may seem like a pious call to inaction, but it is not. Even as we wait for the hand of God to move in our midst, we are called to prepare ourselves for his coming. On the intellectual front, the first and most essential task we face is the need to create a hunger for serious theology within our own ranks. If Evangelical Christians do not want to study these things, we can hardly expect others to do so and any attempt to insist on their importance for the wider church will be undercut by people who claim to be on our side but deny the importance of the issues we are called to face. Nothing is more fatal to the cause of Evangelicals who are fighting for orthodoxy than the intervention of other Evangelicals who cannot see why this matters and who would rather shoot orthodox believers in the foot than support what they are trying to do.

Within the structures of the church our choices are limited, but opting out is the worst choice of all. Synodical government is far from perfect but at least it does enable fresh voices to emerge from the grassroots of the church. Radical groups have shown by their success in getting people elected to key committees that a small number can wield a disproportionate influence, and there is no excuse for us to hold back. At the very least, we should do everything we can to ensure that doctrinal orthodoxy is an essential

---

[96] Matthew 16:24; 2 Timothy 2:12.
[97] Matthew 26:39.

qualification for new appointments, and particularly for senior ones. This can be done through our representatives in General Synod, at the diocesan level, and in parishes that are prepared to use their financial clout in defence of the gospel. Some people think that tactics of this kind are un-Christian, but in a democratic system they are legitimate weapons in a cause which is a matter of life and death for millions. If the gospel is not being heard in our country because Christian people are too polite to preach it, we may be sure that God will soon pass us over and raise up others who will be more actively obedient to his commands.

In any war there are setbacks, and we must be prepared for these. We shall have to live with unsuitable appointments that have already been made, which will be hard for some people to stomach, but it is better to focus on getting right what is to come than on seeking to correct what has already been done. One of the great scandals of the Church of England at the present time is that good candidates for higher appointments are passed over because they are too conservative in their outlook on women's ordination and homosexual practice. This is unjust by any measurement, and there is no reason why we should not be pointing it out whenever we get the opportunity to do so. Another problem is that some young people of conservative views 'mellow' as they get older and rise higher, and often become more of a hindrance to reform than those who start out as liberals. There are undoubtedly people in high office today whose consciences are uneasy because they know that they have sacrificed their principles for the sake of promotion. We must not be surprised if they react against those who are further to their 'right' on the theological spectrum because such people are rebuking them for their unfaithfulness.

Perhaps the most effective way to deal with this tendency to backslide over time is to instil in young people the sense that to be a Christian is to be born again into a new life, and that new life comes as a complete package. You cannot accept Christ emotionally and deny him intellectually, because the two things go together and must receive equal and appropriate emphasis in the Christian life. There is already a considerable body of literature dealing with this problem, but the facts on the ground would suggest that it has not made as much impact as it should have done. Yet only as a generation emerges to whom this matters will change come about. We have to be realistic and remember that however hard we try, we shall never have a perfect church. There will always be those who will deviate from the truth of Christ, and messages like 'Luther got it wrong' or 'Jesus never existed' will continue to make good newspaper headlines, especially at Christmas and Easter. What we need to do is create a climate of opinion in the church which will not tolerate such things if they come from its own accredited ministers, whether they are professors, bishops or parish clergy. If we can reach the point where heterodoxy comes across as aberrant, then we shall have succeeded in producing a church in which the faith of Christ is once more the touchstone of acceptable teaching. When that happens the problem of heresy and the need to do something about it will again be understood and the passion, if not the methods once used to eradicate it, will once again ensure that the church is kept faithful to her Lord and Saviour Jesus Christ.

4.   Schism

4.1.   Division in the church

In theological terms, schism is less serious than heresy because it does not necessarily involve doctrinal questions. In the New Testament there were rival groups within different churches, as we can see from Paul's letters to Corinth and to Rome, but as far as we can tell, these did not lead to any separation. There may have been something approaching a schism in the church mentioned in 3 John, where a man called Diotrephes was contesting the elder's authority, but what was really going on there is unclear and does not seem to have led to an open breach.

There was definitely a schism between the Samaritans and the Jews, because the Samaritans had their own centre of worship on Mt Gerizim which was not subordinate to the Jerusalem temple. Not can there be any doubt that it created a degree of animosity which Jews felt more deeply than the presence of paganism in their midst.[98] The passion which schism can provoke persists to the present day and can still cause more bad feeling than co-existence with other denominations or religions. Thus we find that breakaway Anglican groups in the USA and South Africa (to name but two obvious cases) have a harder time in Anglican circles than do Methodists or Jews, whose right to be different is respected and with whom it is possible, and even politically correct, to engage in ecumenical or inter-faith dialogue. Schismatics on the other hand are usually given the cold shoulder and airbrushed out of the church's consciousness, perhaps because they touch a nerve that other groups do not reach.[99]

---

[98] Jews did not like Greeks and Romans but they seem to have tolerated them better than Samaritans, at least if the New Testament evidence is anything to go by.

[99] It is true that recently the Anglican Communion has reached out to groups like the Reformed Episcopal Church in the USA and the Church of England in South

Historically, the most common cause of schism was the election of a bishop to a see already filled by someone else. This happened at Antioch in 1100, when the victorious crusaders chose one of their own to be the local bishop, in spite of the fact that a Greek prelate loyal to the emperor in Constantinople was already in post. It was a clear breach of canonical order which was repeated throughout the crusader states and ensured that the western and eastern churches would split apart.[100] The next great schism occurred in 1378 when the college of Cardinals, disappointed by the refusal of the newly-elected Pope Urban VI to return to Avignon, left Rome, 'deposed' Urban and elected their own candidate to replace him. Urban refused to accept this decision, and it was not until 1417 that the church was reunited – after several attempts to heal the rift, one of which actually produced a third pope![101]

In the course of the fifteenth century the papacy did all it could to buttress its authority, which had been badly shaken during the schism. The so-called 'conciliar' movement, which had emerged as a compromise solution that promised a more decentralized form of church government, was gradually worn down and finally defeated by Pope Eugenius IV (1431-47), who also tried to heal the schism with the eastern churches. A scheme of reunion was worked out with their representatives at Florence (1439), but although it was superficially accepted for a time, it

---

Africa but relations are still some way from being cordial and they are certainly not recognised as legitimate Anglican churches.

[100] Most histories date the schism to 1054, when legates of the pope excommunicated the patriarch of Constantinople, but this was a personal act which did not touch the wider church. The establishment of separate sees was a different matter though, and when the papacy appointed its own patriarch in Constantinople after the western conquest of the city in 1204, the schism was sealed.

[101] The Church of England has inherited a curious relic of the great schism, in that the bishop of Iona, John Donegan, who remained loyal to Rome when the rest of Scotland joined the schism, fled to London and asked for the protection of the bishop of London. He was able to regain the part of his see which was under English jurisdiction (the Isle of Man) where his successors remain, still claiming the ancient title of 'Sodor and Man', 'Sodor' being the Old Norse name for the Western Isles.

failed in the longer term.[102] However, there were some eastern churches that agreed to it and maintained (or later entered into) communion with Rome. They are now known as 'Uniate' or 'Greek Catholic' churches, but although they were originally meant to heal schism, their existence has proved to be a major stumbling bock towards the reconciliation of the Roman Catholic and Eastern Orthodox churches in modern times.[103] More recently, the Roman Catholic church has had to contend with schisms from time to time, the most important of which has been that of the 'Old Catholics' who refused to accept the proclamation of papal infallibility in 1870.[104] In the eastern churches schism is so common that it sometimes seems almost endemic, though its causes are often political as much as anything else.[105]

The Anglican Communion has not been immune to schism, but it has been of a somewhat different kind. The religious settlement of 1662 produced a large breakaway group, known to us as 'dissenters', who eventually formed themselves into the different 'denominations' with which we are now familiar. As schismatics, they suffered restrictions in social and political life which were not removed until the nineteenth century, but it was always possible

---

[104] It was imposed at Constantinople and might have succeeded had the city been rescued from capture by the Muslim Turks, but after it fell in 1453 that hope vanished, as did the 'reunion' of the churches.

[103] Matters were further complicated by the suppression of the Uniates in many parts of eastern Europe under Communist rule (after 1945). When communism fell, the Uniates re-emerged and have once again become a significant force, especially in Ukraine.

[104] Anglicans have good relations with the Old Catholics and are in limited communion with them.

[105] Some of them have been caused by the refusal of certain groups to accept liturgical changes. This is the case, for example, of the 'Old Believers' in Russia, whose schism dates from 1666, and of the 'Old Calendarists' in Greece, who go back only to 1923. Others are due to disputed jurisdictions, as for example, the Bulgarian exarchate, which was in schism from its foundation in 1870 until 1946, and the church of Macedonia, which was set up in 1959 as a breakaway from the church of Serbia, which still does not recognize it. At the present time, there is a schism in the patriarchate of Jerusalem, where a deposed patriarch (who continues to be recognised by the state of Israel) has been replaced by another, who is not recognised by the secular state. Many other local examples of this kind could also be cited!

for individuals to conform to the state church, and many did so when it suited them. This occasional conformity angered a number of high-church Anglicans but they were powerless to do anything about it, and the phenomenon persists to this day in some places, where there are still people who go to 'church' in the morning and to 'chapel' at night or during the week, without any sense that they are being either inconsistent or 'ecumenical'. The main factor here is that although doctrinal issues were sometimes involved, the seventeenth-century divisions were mostly caused by political factors. The monarch for example is both the supreme governor of the Church of England and also a member of the (Presbyterian) Church of Scotland, even though the two churches are not in communion with each other – an absurd situation which just goes to show that politics and national identity have counted for more in these matters than theology.[106]

More recently, the schisms of the seventeenth and eighteenth centuries have been partly overcome by the progress of ecumenism, which has led to the setting up of joint ministries and worship centres. Resistance to reunion is increasingly confined to certain sections of the clergy (on all sides) and is complicated by the established status of the Church of England, which many dissenters reject and which makes it difficult for Anglicans to be as flexible as they might otherwise be. Elsewhere though, reunion has been possible, particularly in India, where the Church of South India led the way as long ago as 1947.[107]

4.2. The current scene

Meanwhile, schism of yet another kind has appeared among Anglicans and promises to be much more intractable. This involves self-consciously 'Anglican' groups which are not recognized by the

---

[106] Generally speaking, it is the high church members of the Church of England who have insisted on keeping the Presbyterians at arms length, whereas low churchmen have often ignored the issue completely and have worshipped quite happily in the Church of Scotland when they have gone north of the border.

[107] Unfortunately, it took many years for these churches to be fully accepted within the Anglican fold, but that difficulty now appears to have been overcome.

see of Canterbury and are therefore not invited to participate in the decennial Lambeth Conference of bishops.[108] Some of these churches date from the nineteenth century – the Church of England in South Africa and the Reformed Episcopal Church in the USA being the most outstanding examples.[109] More recently though, and largely as a result of liturgical and other changes which have left large, disaffected minorities, schism in some parts of the Anglican Communion has become much more common. The USA leads the way, with as many as twenty independent Anglican bodies now claiming some kind of recognition, many of them receiving it from churches in other parts of the world.[110] The result is that an American congregation which leaves the Episcopal Church and joins a local dissident group is out of communion with Canterbury unless and until that group affiliates with another church, like that of Nigeria, which is in communion with Canterbury! This creates a situation in which the parish of Christ Church in Dead Duck, Alabama can put itself out of communion with the rest of the Anglican world by seceding from its local Episcopal diocese, but re-enter the Anglican Communion by becoming a mission of the Church of Uganda![111] A further complication is that the orders conferred by these schismatic churches are valid. When a bishop of the Church of England in South Africa came to England in 2005 and ordained men for ministry in the diocese of Southwark, their orders were impeccable but they were not recognized by the local bishop because of the irregular way in which they had been conferred.

This is a chaotic situation which most people agree should be avoided, as the recent Windsor Report emphasised. The Report

---

[108] Confusion surrounding the invitation list to Lambeth 2008 indicates that things may be getting even more complicated, as the archbishop of Canterbury has apparently decided not to invite some bishops who are not in any kind of schism. The main reason for this appears to be that their presence might cause scandal to others for moral or political reasons.

[109] There are others, like the Free Church of England, but they are very small and have usually been ignored by everyone else.

[110] Nigeria, Uganda, Rwanda and Bolivia have been especially prominent in this.

[111] The example is fictitious – there is no Dead Duck in Alabama – but there are several churches whose story parallels this one.

has failed to solve the problem however, because it did not take into account the circumstances in which the most recent irregularities have occurred. In virtually every one of these cases, the 'dissidents' have protested that they are the true Anglicans, loyal to the teachings of the church, who have been forced to separate from the ecclesiastical jurisdictions in which they live because the latter have departed from the Anglican norm. At the present time, the key issue is whether homosexual practice can be accepted within the church, a question which typically is answered positively by the local bishop and negatively by those parishes under him that have a strong conservative background. But in this case the parishes have the backing of a resolution passed at the 1998 Lambeth Conference from which their bishop has dissented. This makes it unclear who is being schismatic, and has justified the intervention of bishops from other churches in support of those who have rejected their own bishop's ministry. In the Church of England this type of conflict has not produced schism, but it has occasionally led to the practical equivalent, expressed by the withdrawal of funding from the diocese and the refusal to accept the episcopal ministry of offending diocesans.[112] Muddying the waters still further is the curious decision of the English house of bishops to allow same-sex civil partnerships among the ordained clergy, provided they remain celibate – an absurdity which has left the bishops looking ridiculous and has discredited them in the eyes of most conservatives.[113]

The establishment status of the Church of England makes schism of the American variety virtually impossible, because a parish cannot opt out of the national church. As a result, the bishops have been forced to come up with a way of satisfying dissident minorities who wish to remain Anglican. This has led to the creation of the so-called 'flying bishops', or Provincial Episcopal

---

[112] An English parish can withdraw funding from the diocese because legally its contributions are voluntary!
[113] The bishops have defended their decision on the ground that secular legislation has left them little option, but this is simply not true, as religious bodies can claim (and have so far been granted) exemptions from such legislation on conscientious grounds.

Visitors to give them their proper title, who are appointed by the archbishops of Canterbury and York to provide episcopal oversight and ministry to churches which for one reason or another cannot accept the ministry of their local diocesan. It is an unhappy situation which nobody actively encourages, but it has been made inevitable because the majority in the church's decision-making bodies has departed from traditional Anglican teaching and practice. As in other countries, it is the traditionalists who have the better claim to the name 'Anglican' and the provision of episcopal ministry for them amounts to a tacit (if unwilling) recognition of that fact.

This question may gain in importance in the near future, if plans for the consecration of women bishops in England go ahead. It has already been announced that there will be provision made for those who cannot accept this, but it is important to emphasise that the resulting division, which will be a form of schism, will come about because the majority in the church is not prepared to maintain its traditional teaching and practice. Every effort will be made by that majority to cast the opponents of women bishops in a negative light and to sideline them as much as possible – we have already seen this since the ordination of women presbyters began in 1994. No doubt people will be careful not to use words like 'sectarian' and 'schismatic' too publicly, but it will be hard not to give that impression. If a 'schism' of this kind develops in England, it will not be because a minority has broken away from the church but because the current majority in it has not remained faithful to the teaching of Scripture, a point that needs to be made with as much clarity (and charity!) as possible. Saying this will not be popular, but the truth seldom is and we shall be reminded again that superficial unity is no substitute for substantial agreement in matters of faith and practice.

The dilemma facing Anglicans in such situations is that while those in favour of the innovations have a parliamentary-style majority in General Synod and enjoy the sympathy of most of the media, their opponents have the stronger arguments and the support of other churches around the world. The situation is made worse by the fact that there is no way of imposing a common stance on member churches of the Anglican Communion so that it is hard to say how far one member church can go before it is no longer recognised by the others. The American Episcopal Church operates independently and has pushed the boundaries as far as it can, but at the same time it wants to be part of the Anglican Communion, which is difficult if it is unwilling to defer to the wishes of other member churches that object to some of its decisions. As a result, it has voted itself into schism almost without realising it – a strange situation, but one which a conflict between the demands of local autonomy on the one hand and catholic communion on the other is almost bound to produce sooner or later.

5.   Apostasy

5.1.   Abandoning the Christian faith altogether

The intra-Anglican schisms of recent years have often been provoked by a belief that the official church or some of its bishops have apostatised from the Christian faith. That is a grave charge, and demands a careful examination of what apostasy is. The word was initially used to refer to those who had made a profession of faith and then backslidden. There were people like that in the New Testament, which contains warnings of the danger of apostasy that suggest it was a real fear among the early Christians.[114] Later on, there were many people who recanted their faith in times of persecution and then sought readmission to the church once the danger was past, though whether they can properly be called 'apostates' is less clear. The general tendency was to accept them back after proper repentance, though this solution was highly unpopular in North Africa and helped to produce the Donatist schism soon after Christianity was legalised.

The classic case of apostasy was that of the Emperor Julian, who was brought up as a Christian but rejected it when he reached the throne in 361. He died in the Persian wars only two years later, so his apostasy never had much effect, but it has always been remembered (and denounced) by the church.[115] In the middle ages there were many thousands of nominal Christians who apostatised to Islam when their countries were overrun by the Arabs, though Muslims did relatively little to encourage this until after the crusades.[116] In later centuries there would be a steady stream of

---

[114] For the existence of apostates, see 2 Timothy 4:10. For the warnings, see Matthew 13:38-40; Hebrews 6:4-6; Jude 18-19.

[115] Conversely, of course, Julian has become an object of fascination among many who reject Christianity in modern times.

[116] The early Muslims were quite tolerant of Christians and often preferred them to remain such because they could be more highly taxed. After the crusades though, the danger of allowing a 'fifth column' of Christians to survive in a Muslim state

apostates of this kind, some of whom were slaves captured in Western Europe and deported to North Africa, though they have been largely lost to view in the modern world. The conversion of Christians to Islam and other religions has continued on a modest scale, but as this is part and parcel of a general secularization of the once-Christian west, it is less commented-on than it would have been in the past.

Within the Christian world, apostasy came to mean the renunciation of a religious order which the person concerned had professed. Monks and nuns who ran away to get married were called apostates – the most famous examples being Peter Abelard in the twelfth century and Martin Luther in the sixteenth! The term can still be used in that sense within the Roman Catholic Church, though nowadays there are recognized procedures for leaving a religious order and those who do so are seldom stigmatised in this way.

Among Anglicans, apostasy has occurred from time to time but it has rarely attracted much popular attention. The most notable exception to this was the famous assize sermon preached by John Keble at Oxford on 14 July 1833, in which he described the emancipation of dissenters and Roman Catholics and the consequent ending of the traditional link between church and state in parliament as nothing less than 'national apostasy'. Keble's criticism of the establishment, which rejected his suggestion that it had abandoned the Christian faith, was generally regarded as extreme, but his sermon was powerful enough to lead to the creation of the Tractarian movement, which became the nucleus of what we now call Anglo-Catholicism.[117]

Dramatic disavowals of Christianity by Anglicans have remained uncommon, but the situation has been greatly complicated by the position and pastoral practice of the church. By practising indiscriminate baptism and demanding little or nothing of the baptised, Anglicans have invited widespread 'apostasy' (if

---

increased the pressure on them to convert to Islam.

[117] Eventually some of its adherents, most famously John Henry Newman (1801-90), joined the Roman Catholic Church.

that is the right word for it) as generations of theoretically baptised people have grown up with little or no Christian knowledge and have never taken the slightest interest in the church. Many others have received basic Christian instruction at some point in their lives but either have not followed it through or else have dropped out along the way. However, the fact that so many of them declare themselves to be 'Christians' on census forms makes it difficult to call them 'apostates', since they have not consciously rejected Christianity even if they do not actively profess it either. In England we now have a situation in which more than seventy percent of the population claims to be 'Christian' although only about a third of these have any connection with a church. Atheists, agnostics and secular humanists are well aware of this of course, and discount these figures, claiming that in reality England is a thoroughly secular country where Christians are a tiny minority. The government and the media seem to agree with this assessment, with the result that holidays like Christmas and Easter are largely devoid of Christian content.[118] Even if the true situation is not as dire as this, there is no doubt that for the majority of the population Christianity is more a matter of passive acceptance than of active commitment, something which creates a huge pastoral dilemma for the church.

One point to notice here is that apostasy has usually been an individual thing – it is particular people who renounce their faith, not whole churches that fall away. The possibility that the latter might happen is not denied in the New Testament, as can be seen from the seven churches of Asia in the book of Revelation, and the reformers of the sixteenth century certainly believed that it had occurred. To them, the ancient churches of Alexandria and Antioch had both left the fold, and so had Rome, though precisely when and how they had abandoned the faith remained somewhat unclear.[119] Today however, very few people would describe these

---

[118] On Good Friday 2007 the only mention of the death of Christ on TV came on the soap opera *Eastenders*, and this was only because Dot failed to go to church as she usually did on that day and the vicar had to be called in to see what was wrong!
[119] Antioch and Alexandria presumably fell away by rejecting the council of Chalcedon in 451. Many Protestant apologists traced Rome's apostasy to the

churches as 'apostate' and the ecumenical climate of our times has virtually ensured that it will no longer be used of other Christian bodies, however much they may differ from each other.

5.2. The current crisis

The recent accusations of apostasy levelled against the American Episcopal Church, and against some other Anglican bodies as well, are of a different order. These Anglicans have not formally abandoned Christianity and insist that the radical decisions they have taken are a necessary development of the faith in modern circumstances. Are they right?

First of all, it must be said that a radical or non-traditional decision is not by itself a sign of apostasy. At the time of the Reformation, many Protestant churches abolished the monarchical episcopate and others rejected infant baptism. Both moves were radical innovations at the time, but however much others objected to them, they never accused the radicals of apostasy. The abolition of episcopacy, where it occurred, was largely a political act with little doctrinal significance. The rejection of infant baptism was originally thought to imply a denial of the doctrine of original sin, which is why the first Anabaptists were frequently accused of Pelagianism, but eventually it was accepted that this was a mistake and that a different sacramental practice did not necessarily involve an abandonment of orthodox Christianity.

Where does the American Episcopal Church stand in relation to this? The main issue at stake is the fact that the Episcopal Church has ordained practising homosexuals and even consecrated one as a bishop. Is this a breach of Christian doctrine which amounts to apostasy? Supporters of the Episcopal Church naturally reject such a conclusion, even when they accept that not everyone agrees with them on the issue and that objections to their decision may have some validity. They think that it ought to be possible to discuss matters of this kind within the Anglican fold,

---

Hildebrandine reforms of the eleventh century, but why it took more than 400 years for anyone to leave the apostate church was left unexplained!

without threatening to anathematize opponents and short-circuit further discussion. On the other side, their opponents argue that the question of homosexuality raises profound issues of world-view which are shaped by our most fundamental doctrines – in this case, the doctrine of creation. Sexuality may have many functions and expressions, but at the heart of the two-sex reality we live in lies the reproductive capacity of the human race. If homosexuality is regarded as 'normal', then the purposeful nature of God's creation, which is a fundamental biblical and creedal doctrine, is effectively denied. Whether this is neo-gnosticism or neo-paganism scarcely matters; either way, it is a rejection of the Christian faith and therefore apostasy.

If the argument from creation stands, then the leaders of the American Episcopal Church and those who agree with them are indeed apostate, because they have rejected one of the cornerstones of our faith. It is sometimes said that redemption is more important than creation and that in Christ all things are reconciled, but this sets up a false opposition between two equally-important aspects of the truth. If Christians do tend to emphasise redemption more than creation, it is not in a way that denies the fundamental givenness of the created order! In Christ we are a new creation, called by God to live the kinds of lives which he intended for Adam and Eve before they fell, not something radically different. We cannot achieve that goal in this life, but in preparation for it we are called to put to death the lusts of the flesh, including those that veer in a homosexual direction, or in a heterosexual one outside the bounds of marriage. Students of the ancient pagan world know that the worship of the gods was often linked to immoral sexual practices, and so it is not illogical to suggest that the modern recurrence of these things is a re-emergence of some form of paganism. Those who pray to 'Mother Jesus' feminise God and do nothing to allay the suspicion that a new fertility cult has come into being, using the language of the Christian faith but denying its substance. Whether we like it or not, those who do such things have moved out of the Christian church into a new religion, and that is the ultimate sign of apostasy.

6.   Orthodoxy and the future of Anglicanism

6.1.   Orthodoxy and Anglicanism

Heresy, schism and apostasy differ from one another, but all three ultimately derive their meaning from the concept of 'orthodoxy'. Orthodoxy may not always be clear-cut or easy to define, but it exists and it is the duty of the church to teach and defend it. The institutions of the Anglican Communion have authority and validity only to the extent that they do this; if they fail, their claims will be discredited and they will be consigned to oblivion just as the ancient heresies have been.

Anglican orthodoxy has two distinct aspects, the first of which may be described as universal or 'catholic'. All Christian churches believe in the supreme authority of a divinely-inspired Scripture, even if there are some (relatively minor) differences about the extent of the canon, the nature of divine inspiration and the place to be given to those external sources that we group together as 'tradition'. These are important questions, but failure to resolve them to everyone's satisfaction does not take away the fact that the Bible remains the central foundation of Christian doctrine. The ancient creeds, in particular the one we call the Nicene Creed are also generally agreed to be an accurate summary of biblical teaching and are accepted as such throughout the Christian world. By adopting them, Anglicans are subscribing to an ecumenical consensus, which makes dissent from them all the more serious when it occurs. For an Anglican theologian or bishop to say that the Bible is wrong is not simply to go against the teaching of his own church, but against the teaching of Christendom as a whole, and our perceived failure to discipline people who do this compromises our standing in the wider ecumenical world. There is nothing more embarrassing than having to explain to representatives of other churches why we put up with heresy and unbelief, even at the highest levels of the church. The musings of an outrageously liberal bishop may not affect us much at the personal level, but in the eyes of other Christians such things compromise our integrity as a church and make them wonder what kind of people they are dealing with when they talk to us.

The second dimension of Anglican orthodoxy may be described as particular or 'local', in that it applies only to our own church. It can be found in the formularies of the Church of England – the Thirty-nine Articles of Religion, the Homilies, the Book of Common Prayer and the Ordinal. These documents have not been explicitly adopted by every member church of the Communion but it is hard to see how any church could call itself 'Anglican' without being at least in general sympathy with their teaching. There is even some precedent for regarding them as essential to Anglican identity, because in 1634 they were forced on the Church of Ireland for precisely that reason. The Irish Church already had its own articles of religion, which in many respects were superior to those of the Church of England, but it was told that communion with Canterbury meant adopting the English articles as the doctrinal standard and it complied.[120] After the American revolution, the newly-independent Protestant Episcopal Church also adopted the Articles, albeit in a revised form which took account of the political separation which had occurred.[121] The history of the various prayer books is more complicated, but with some exceptions, most Anglican churches today look back to the 1662 Prayer Book one way or another and if a liturgical style of worship is to remain central to Anglican identity it is hard to see how that could be abandoned without losing our unity altogether.[122] In the Church of England these standards are enshrined in law and cannot be altered by any authority except that of Parliament. This is not a guarantee that they will continue in force, but it does at least erect a substantial hurdle against would-be revisionists. Experience suggests that Parliament would be unlikely to alter or abolish them if there was a significant voice within the church that opposed such

---

[120] The Irish articles were not abrogated but fell into disuse.

[121] Article 21 was dropped and Article 37 seriously modified. Less satisfactorily, Article 8 was revised to omit any mention of the Athanasian Creed.

[122] The Scottish and American Episcopal churches are the main exception to this; they both rely more on the 1549 book and its abortive revision in 1637. Modern liturgical revision has created a major problem though, since in many cases individual churches have gone their own way, often producing so many different forms that it is hard to say there is any unity even within a given local church.

a move, as there certainly would be.

The main difficulty with Anglican orthodoxy is that the standards used to define it all date from the sixteenth and seventeenth centuries. The world has moved on since then, and not even the staunchest defender of the Reformation settlement would claim that nothing has changed. It is not difficult to see that some of the Articles are no longer relevant or applicable and nobody would suggest that they are. We do not now want to insist that councils must be called together by the state authorities (as Article 21 indicates) and Article 37 does not apply outside England. However we must not allow obvious anachronisms like these to be cited as proof that the Articles as a whole have lost their importance. What they have to say about the Bible, about justification by faith, about the sacraments, the church and so on remains as meaningful today as it was when they were first composed. If they require revision it is because they do not say enough – not because they say too much or because they say the wrong thing.

Having said that, it is becoming increasingly clear that new challenges demand new statements of faith that can address them adequately. The homosexual question is an obvious case in point. The Thirty-nine Articles never mentioned anything like that because everyone was agreed on the subject, as was still the case only a generation or so ago. Now that the traditional view has been questioned though, it may be desirable for the church to formulate a binding statement about it so that it can resolve the difficulties created by recent events in North America and prevent their recurrence in the future. Slowly, it seems that the organs of worldwide Anglicanism are working their way towards some form of 'covenant' which will commit member churches to a common policy. It is also possible that there will soon be an Anglican Catechism, rather like the *Catechism of the Catholic Church*, which may serve as a kind of handbook and guide to Anglican doctrine, though how widely it will be accepted is impossible to say.

The problem is that documents of this kind are bound to split the existing structures one way or another. Something produced by the liberal wing of the church will be rejected by the conservatives, and vice versa, but a compromise between the two is liable to be rejected by both – for different reasons! Nobody can guarantee that every member church would adopt whatever was proposed, and it is certain that there would be a wide latitude of interpretation within several of them. In England such a document could not be used to define the doctrine of the church in a legal forum because unless it were to be passed by Parliament it would have no such authority. Other churches have different constitutional structures but many of them have similar internal controls which would circumscribe the uses to which such documents could be put. As things stand at the moment, Anglican orthodoxy must continue to be defended on the basis of the traditional formularies, although this should not prevent us from exploring new avenues for the future. Development in these matters is slow and we should not expect to see radical changes anytime soon, but it is always worth creating a precedent for others to fall back on if and when such changes become a real possibility. Setting the tone for what should be done is just as important as actually doing it, since only when a reasonable consensus emerges will further doctrinal definition occur.

Some people will argue that the Anglican way is a polite one, that accusations of heresy and the like should not be made in our churches and that we ought to be dedicated to comprehending as wide a variety of Christian faith and practice as possible. There is certainly something to be said for this approach, and the decorous way in which the primates of the Anglican Communion go about their business is a model of which we can be proud. Nevertheless, we must recognise that there are serious problems that will not go away and must be resolved if the Anglican witness is to survive. The experience of the American Episcopal Church is a reminder that survival is not inevitable; as it has lurched to the theological 'left' so it has lost members at an alarming rate, and is now only about half as strong as it was a generation ago. If that trend continues it will disappear sometime late in this century, if it does not implode long before that. The same is true, though less obviously, of the Church of England and of the Anglican churches in the developed world. For example, when electoral rolls were first compiled in 1921, the diocese of Ely mustered about 39,000 names out of a total population of 300,000 – the lowest figure in the Church of England at that time. Today, the population of the diocese has more than doubled (to about 665,000) but the numbers on electoral rolls have fallen to no more that 18,500, or less than half of what they were in 1921.[123] In other words, the active membership of the Church of England in Ely has declined from 13% of the population to 3% in two generations and is set to shrink even further. Some individual parishes are growing, but they are the ones that have taken a firm line against heterodox doctrine and practice. That the survival of traditional orthodoxy in the developing world cannot simply be attributed to sociological conditions is amply demonstrated by the case of Sydney (Australia), a first-world diocese that continues to grow and stands as an open (though unintended) rebuke to those who believe that the church must change its views if it is going to appeal to modern people.

6.2. Form and substance

Anglicanism has always been characterised by the fine balance which the Reformers struck between the form and the substance of Christian faith. They embraced the most sophisticated Protestant doctrine of their time but managed to express it in a way that retained as much of the classical forms of the church and its worship as were compatible with the necessary changes that they made. The result was a synthesis which is widely admired and that many people in other European countries wish could have been implemented there as well. If France or Germany had been able to construct a similar church, the devastating civil wars which they suffered might have been avoided and the enduring rift between Protestant and Catholic overcome. In the early seventeenth century, people like King James I actually believed that Anglicanism was the answer to the reunion of Christendom, and not simply of the Western part of it.[124] Even as late as the mid-

---

[123] In 2005-6 the number fell by 1000, at which rate there will be no church left by 2025. The only consolation, such as it is, is that Ely is no longer at the bottom of the league table. Birmingham, Bradford, Bristol, Coventry, Hereford, Leicester, Newcastle, Peterborough, Portsmouth, Ripon and Leeds, Southwell and Nottingham and Truro are now all worse off (leaving the exceptional cases of Sodor and Man and the diocese in Europe out of the count).

[124] See W. B. Patterson, *King James VI and I and the reunion of Christendom*

twentieth century, Anglicans played a significant role in the ecumenical movement because our church was the one that others could most easily relate to one way or another.

Today, that enviable position has gone, and this is almost entirely because of the doctrinal implosion which has occurred within the Anglican world itself. One of the main reasons for this is that the delicate balance between form and substance has been lost, and the responsibility for this must be laid at the door of the liberal Catholics who dominate so much of official Anglicanism today. What we now have is a church where people who deny almost every major Christian doctrine prance about in pseudo-medieval costume claiming to be 'bishops in the church of God' merely because the right people have laid hands on them in canonically approved ceremonies. The inadequacy of this ecclesiology was highlighted when a practising homosexual was elected and duly consecrated as a bishop in the American Episcopal church, but he was by no means the first non-Christian to attain such high office, as the careers of John Spong and the late James Pike demonstrate. It is ironic that Roman Catholics and Eastern Orthodox people who are supposed to be the most appreciative of such ceremonies have been among those most scandalised by them, perhaps because they understand that there is more to being a teacher of the Word of God than wearing a fancy hat.

Sadly, it must be said that for two or three generations now, liberal Catholics within the Anglican fold have been progressively hollowing out its doctrine whilst at the same time insisting on its ceremonies. It would be hard to find anyone who has been denied ordination for failing to believe in the bodily resurrection of Jesus, but many ordinands can testify to the problems they have had with their bishops when they have refused to wear a stole – as if the piece of cloth around their necks was more important than those left behind in the empty tomb! The recent Windsor Report is a magnificent example of how this inversion of priorities has taken over the Communion generally. The authors of that report could not bring themselves to denounce the promotion of homosexuality

---

(Cambridge: Cambridge University Press, 1997).

in the United States and Canada as heretical (though they were forced to accept that it had become 'divisive'), but they were firm in their condemnation of those bishops from around the world who rushed to the defence of the orthodox opponents of revisionism in North America, as if crossing diocesan boundaries were as serious an offence as denying the gospel. More recently, the bishop of Southwark saw fit to revoke the licence of one of his clergy who had called a South African bishop to ordain men for a church plant (which Southwark had repeatedly refused to do) but has done nothing to discipline the liberal clergy in his diocese, not least the dean of his cathedral, who has publicly compared orthodox Christians to the Taliban. Only in a climate where form has been allowed to trump substance could such things happen, and the consequences have brought the Anglican Communion to the brink of schism.

6.3. Word and Spirit

Another problem, which originates at the opposite end of the theological spectrum, is the danger of divorcing the Word from the Spirit. Here again, classical Anglicanism is noted for its balance. Its worship is impregnated with the Word of God, but that Word serves as a catalyst for experiencing the presence of the Holy Spirit. Those who know the Spirit in their lives feed on the Word and grow as Christians in a balanced and comprehensive way, because the rhythm of Anglican liturgy forces us to consider every aspect of our faith and test ourselves against it. We are not left to the mercies (or the predilections!) of our ministers, but are guided by an overall plan designed to ensure healthy growth in the body of Christ. Yet here again the balance between these things has been lost, this time in supposedly conservative circles as much as in liberal ones. At one end of the spectrum are Anglo-Catholics who believe in a doctrine of 'baptismal regeneration' which suggests that anyone sprinkled with holy water has received the Holy Spirit and is thereby born again. Evangelicals everywhere reject this idea – after all, Hitler was baptised and who would claim that he was a born-again Christian? Unfortunately the idea that a person is a church member on the strength of baptism has led to a situation in which we are expected to treat all baptised people as fellow-believers, regardless of what they actually think. Quite apart from the millions of nominal Christians who were baptised in infancy and have completely forgotten about it since, there are many within the churches who have no idea what Christianity is about and make no attempt to put it into practice in their lives. For them, churchgoing is a Sunday social event and not much more. Far worse than that, there are ordained clergy who do not preach the gospel, or even understand what it is. An outstanding example of this was recently provided by the dean of St Albans, who denounced the Christian doctrine of the atonement on Radio 4 shortly before Easter 2007 and was publicly rebuked – at some length – by the bishop of Durham among others. Yet the dean carries on as if nothing has happened, and there are many more like him who do the same.

At the other end of the spectrum there are people from an Evangelical background who have also dissociated the Word from the Spirit. Instead of believing that the work of the Holy Spirit is to illuminate our understanding of the Word of God, they maintain that he now comes to us to give us further revelation, which is often so personal and subjective that it is hard to know what to make of it. In some cases, people who make these claims are being helped to overcome some problem in their lives and we must be duly sensitive to this.[125] But to preach that there can be a direct revelation from God which supplements the Bible is heretical – that is what Muhammad and Joseph Smith claimed, and it is clearly not Christian. I once went to a meeting where the speaker, a well-known Evangelical clergyman, used Ezekiel 37 to tell us that it was God's will for us, the dry bones of the church, to *sing* in tongues that very evening. There is nothing wrong with singing in tongues if that is what the Holy Spirit wants us to do, but to claim that Ezekiel 37 teaches this and that all Christians must experience it is not merely outrageous – it is blasphemous! Nothing in the Scriptures says anything like that; on the contrary, the Apostle Paul

---

[125] The Alpha Course often highlights people who have been transformed from a life of immorality and self-destruction, and we must respect this. Problems arise when the Course tries to insist on its own interpretation of the work of the Holy Spirit, which appears to be divorced from any serious connection to the Word of God.

tells us that the gifts of the Spirit are given to individuals chosen to receive them for the purpose of building up the church. As far as he was concerned, speaking in tongues was neither universal nor compulsory, so how can singing in them be so regarded?

Nonsense like this is now widespread in Evangelical circles where it dilutes the power of Christian doctrine, because it is virtually impossible to say anything to someone who claims to be 'filled with the Spirit' in this way. Why study theology if all you need is a laying on of hands to receive the gift(s)? There are now churches where people come before the service for the 'worship' and stay afterwards for the 'ministry', as if the service itself were a hiatus between these two things. The superficiality of all this is amply demonstrated by the fact that some of the leaders of this movement have been attracted to the Eastern Orthodox churches because of their mystical use of sound, colour and smell in worship. Doctrinal differences do not bother them because they never had any clear doctrine to begin with.[126]

6.4. Biblical interpretation and hermeneutics

For Anglicans, Christian doctrine is rooted in the Bible, and so the way we read the sacred text is of the utmost importance for the future development of our church's sense of orthodoxy. The archbishop of Canterbury has recently encouraged us to study this question more deeply by a process of 'listening', without specifying what that is supposed to mean. Some idea of what it might involve can be gleaned from a recent series of lectures which he has published, entitled *Tokens of trust.*[127] Listening to Scripture is a community activity, to be done in the company of the whole church, past and present. This is a promising start but we must be careful not to fall into the trap of thinking that Scripture is essentially a springboard for mystical reflection about God. There is certainly more to the Christian life than expounding the text of

---

[126] To their credit, many Eastern Orthodox leaders are deeply suspicious of such 'converts' to their branch of the faith.

[127] R. Williams, *Tokens of trust* (Norwich: Canterbury Press, 2007). See especially pp. 122-6.

the Bible, but that does not mean that biblical exposition is not fundamental to our spiritual experience. On the contrary, its teaching must guide and direct our minds as we seek to interpret and extend our experience. Especially worrying is the tendency to seize on the phrase 'verbal inerrancy' (or some variation of that) as something which is unacceptable. Of course it is always possible to express this idea in a way which leads to absurdities, but what it affirms is that the Bible is a trustworthy account of God's revelation to us and must be treated as such. It makes propositional statements of fact and truth which we must accept, using what is clear in the text as a guide to interpreting what is more obscure. Unfortunately recent experience suggests that by denying this fundamental principle, leaders of our church are trying to interpret away what they do not like and in the process turn the Christian faith inside out.

A lot of the argument about verbal accuracy turns on the issue of the Bible as history. The assumption is often made that modern secular historians are by and large objective analysts of the data whereas the biblical writers and their modern apologists distort the facts in the interests of their own religious propaganda. In answering this, it might be helpful to take a modern example first and extrapolate from there to the ancient world. Nobody doubts that since 1492 Christianity has spread to the far corners of the globe or that this expansion was closely connected to the great European empires, from which most of the missionaries who preached the gospel originally came. Christians may see the hand of God in this and rejoice that secular forces were used to bring millions of people to a knowledge of Christ. Others though may take a different line and criticise the churches for their complicity in what they see as a barbarous and unjustified display of naked power. Who is right? Some of the details remain obscure, but the basic facts are there for all to see and the amount of information available is overwhelming. That is not a problem, but the way in which these facts are interpreted is. Many variant readings of them are possible, but most Christians will probably be attracted to the view that God was at work in a positive way, even if not everything the missionaries did can be commended. However, the other point of view also exists and for atheists it may seem to be more plausible. When speaking to them, Christians may resort to secular arguments to bolster their case, such as the fact that Christianity has spread much more rapidly since the departure of the colonialists than it did before, but even so, what they say will clearly come from a perspective of faith. In the end, the presuppositions which one brings to the situation will influence the conclusions one draws as much as any of the individual facts, and the resulting 'history' will turn out to be less objective than was once thought.

If we move from that example to the Bible, we find that the ancient Hebrew scribes wrote history from a very particular point of view. The great powers of those days were the empires of Egypt, Assyria, Babylon, Persia and Rome, but these play only secondary parts in the biblical narrative. The main focus is on Jerusalem and its rulers, which is rather like writing a history of Europe focussing on Luxembourg. Is this justified? A secular historian of the ancient world is almost bound to say that it is not, but a Christian cannot be so certain. After all, if we look at the Middle East today, it is quite possible to understand what is going on there without knowing much about Rameses II or Ashurbanipal. But no-one will get far without taking Abraham and Moses into consideration, even though they could not have built a pyramid between them. Of all the nations of antiquity, only Israel survives today in a recognisable form, which surely says something about its importance. As Christians we do not have to be embarrassed about reading the evidence from the standpoint of our faith, since it is the survival of that faith which is the one thing that links us to that distant past and makes it meaningful in the modern world. As with the modern missionary movement, many of the details remain obscure but the broad picture is clear enough and the scholar who claims to have disproved the Bible by some theory or other needs to be very careful about making such statements. The ancients were not fools and very few of them would have gone cheerfully to their deaths if they knew (or strongly suspected) that what they believed was historically untrue. Furthermore, unlike the case of modern missions, only a very limited amount of data is now available to test the various theories which are put forward and much of what is said, even about the early church, is necessarily conjectural. There is no need to believe a word of it and good reason to be sceptical – after all, if Luke's account of the spread of the gospel was wrong, why did nobody notice until Ferdinand Christian Baur came along in the early nineteenth century?

Everything said about the Bible is an interpretation of some kind and therefore 'biased' one way or another. The New Testament is itself an interpretation of the Jewish Scriptures that expounds them as having been fulfilled in Christ, and we know that it was rejected by many Jews even when it was first written. Christians have always had to argue their case and have usually succeeded in making it defensible without sacrificing their intellectual integrity. Recently the issue of biblical interpretation has been complicated by introducing the word 'hermeneutic(s)' which is roughly synonymous with 'interpretation' but has come to mean something rather more technical. A hermeneutic is a comprehensive theory or pattern according to which particular passages of the Bible are read. For example, an interpreter of Scripture trying to decide what the Bible has to say about women and their ministry in the church will look at passages like 1 Timothy 2:11-15 and try to decide what they mean. But someone who adopts a feminist hermeneutic will read the entire Bible from that perspective. That involves interpreting what is recorded about almost every woman in the text as relevant to this question, as well as every sign of male domination or 'patriarchy'. Where this can lead is shown by the recent assertion that Mary Magdalene was the first apostle (because she was the first to see the risen Christ) and that women are therefore entitled to become church leaders and bishops! To people who do not appreciate the nature of the hermeneutic being adopted this sounds like nonsense, but to those who follow the logic of a feminist hermeneutic it seems to make perfect sense.

The temptation to impose an alien thought system on Scripture goes back to the first centuries of the church and has taken different forms over the years. Quite apart from 'gnosticism' there was the tendency to allegorise the text. At first allegory was used only to interpret the difficult passages of the Bible, meaning those parts where the literal meaning of the words seemed to be inadequate or impossible for some reason. It was particularly popular as a way of interpreting the parables of Jesus and became the standard way of reading the Song of Songs in the Old Testament. As time went on however, it was extended to other things, so that virtually the whole of the Old Testament could be spiritualised away by finding hidden meanings behind the text.

It is often thought that allegory dominated Christian thinking until the sixteenth century, but that is not true. In the middle ages there were periodic revivals of learning when prominent clerics did their best to restore the literal meaning of the Bible. Interestingly enough, a leading role in this was played by Englishmen. The names of Stephen Langton, Thomas of Chobham, Herbert of Bosham and the various monks of St Victor[128] are not widely known today, but they were largely responsible for developing a method of reading the Bible which eschewed allegory and concentrated on the grammatical sense of the text. John Wycliffe came later and pursued a different career, but he also belonged to this tradition. In the sixteenth century this whole movement was transformed by the rediscovery of the importance of the original manuscripts. Some medieval scholars had consulted the rabbis about the meaning of Old Testament texts but very few of them had a working knowledge of Greek. The arrival of scholars fleeing a dying Byzantium changed that and by the time Erasmus (1466-1536) came on the scene, knowledge of Greek was more common. In 1516 he published a critical edition of the New Testament along with a revised Latin translation and the study of Scripture has not been the same since. Erasmus' influence in England was very great and affected all sides in the religious controversies which erupted later on. Thomas Cranmer and Thomas More were both in his debt and his *Paraphrases* of the Gospels were among the few works which every Anglican clergyman was expected to possess.

What Erasmus encouraged was the study of the Bible in its original languages according to their grammatical sense. He was so successful that until very recently any other approach to the Bible was regarded as unscientific and unacceptable. Erasmus' model was supplemented by John Calvin, who set it in a comprehensive theological framework integrating exegesis (the study of the original texts and their meaning), exposition (the theological

---

[128] St Victor was a monastery in Paris, but many of its leading monks, including Richard and Andrew, were Englishmen.

synthesis) and application (the preaching of the Word to the church). His *Commentaries* were his exegesis, his *Institutes* were his exposition and his *Sermons* were his application. In the reign of Elizabeth I they were translated into English and became the staple diet of theological students in the universities, along with the writings of other theologians who essentially followed his method.[129] Not everyone agreed with Calvin's conclusions and some of them sparked lively debates, but his method took root and remains the cornerstone of Protestant theology to this day. The Anglican world is firmly in his debt and his principles have dominated Anglican biblical studies, regardless of churchmanship.

Erasmus and Calvin both took it for granted that the Bible was essentially a historical record of real events and they read it accordingly. They were not naive when it came to matters like the six-day creation and were prepared to accept that much in the text was meant to be understood symbolically or poetically, but this was because they believed that the literal sense of the text demanded it. They never supposed that ancient writers were trying to deceive the public or present as 'history' something which was essentially mythical. That idea first emerged in the seventeenth century in the work of the early Deists – many of them also English or Irish as it happens – but nobody supposed that the Deists were orthodox Christians and their rather jejune theories were easily discounted. It was not until the nineteenth century that scepticism of this sort became widespread within the Christian community and that happened in Germany, not in England. In fact, Anglican theologians distinguished themselves by combating German biblical criticism and the famous Cambridge trio of J. B. Lightfoot, B. F. Westcott and F. J. A. Hort are still remembered for the solid work which they did in this area.

Nevertheless, the secularisation of the universities and the growth of anti-establishment feeling associated with the rise of liberal nonconformity led to the introduction of German 'higher

---

[129] Not all Calvin's Sermons were published. Some are still in manuscript form in Geneva and others have been lost, but those that were available in print were translated.

criticism' into British theological faculties in the 1890s and by the end of the First World War it had become the dominant school of thought. A scholarly and conservative Anglican tradition continued to exist however, and was represented among both Anglo-Catholics and Evangelicals, who had a common interest in opposing it. Anglo-Catholics tended to concentrate on theological questions, mainly because of their interest in the early church period, whereas Evangelicals were so Bible-centred that they pushed the notion of *sola Scriptura* almost to the point of ignoring theology altogether. It is one of the tragedies of modern Anglicanism that at a time when the two sides needed the contribution the other had to make, they moved in different worlds and preferred to attack each other rather than co-operate. The result was that the middle ground was left to the liberals who could speak to the 'broad church' constituency and attract moderate opinion from both of the more extreme wings of Anglicanism.

Today the Anglo-Catholic tradition represented by people like the late J. N. D. Kelly and Eric Mascall has fallen on hard times. The Evangelical tradition is stronger and continues to produce good work on the Bible, but its aversion to theology has not served it well. An ill-informed polemic against so-called 'Calvinism' has divided them and made it difficult for evangelical organisations to affirm a consistently Reformed theology. Over the years many Evangelicals have been lost to the orthodox cause, either because they have failed to understand the importance of theology and fallen for interpretations of the biblical text which are inconsistent with Christian belief, or because they have been attracted by philosophical ideas which have led them into various kinds of 'new hermeneutic' which owe more to German philosophers like Martin Heidegger than to the Bible. Instead of offering a viable alternative, they have been sitting ducks for all the latest trends, from the neo-orthodoxy of Karl Barth to liberation theology, the 'new perspective' on Paul, feminism and a host of other things. By supposing that they could do without the traditional Reformed hermeneutic, Evangelicals have fallen for an eclectic mix of ideas and so they usually come across sounding naive and unconvincing. With few exceptions, no department in Evangelical theological colleges is weaker than the theological one, or in greater need of a thorough overhaul.

6.5. Theological renewal

The key to a renewal of orthodox Anglican theology lies in the recovery of its classical tradition. This must begin with the theology of the early church, an area in which conservative Anglo-Catholics excelled until quite recently. Without a thorough grounding in patristic theology it is impossible to understand what Christian orthodoxy is or why it matters. One of the most exciting developments in recent years has been a rediscovery of the biblical foundations of patristic thought, which ought to appeal to the Evangelical constituency. It is now clear that the Fathers of the Church wrote extensively on the Bible and that their commentaries were much more literal in their interpretation than most people have realised. The Ancient Christian Commentary on Scripture (ACCS) has brought this out very clearly and promises to become a major resource for the next generation.[130] It has been a best-seller in the USA and has already been translated into languages like Spanish, Russian and Chinese, but it has not found a UK publisher, which gives us some indication of the parlous state of the discipline in this country. In the ACCS the Fathers come across as skilled exegetes and thinkers who argued the Christian case against the best minds of their time – and won. They were clearly orthodox but far from uniform in their approach, which gives the lie to the view that orthodoxy was a conspiracy to impose a minority view on the church as a whole.

The next thing needed is a recovery of the Reformation period and its theology. There is a rich tradition here and much of it is readily available to anyone who cares to look for it, but few do. No-one should be allowed to graduate from an Anglican theological college or be accepted for ordination who has not had a thorough grounding in the classical formularies of the church in which they want to minister, yet that is almost universally the case at the present time. This is not a party issue but something which goes to the heart of our identity. It is not necessary to agree with everything the Reformers said or did, but not to understand them is

---

[130] It is edited by Thomas C. Oden, an American Methodist theologian and is published by Inter-Varsity Press in the USA.

inexcusable and those who are not prepared to defend them, at least in general terms, should not be training for Anglican ministry.

The study of modern theology is also important but it belongs in third place. For a start, it is not possible to understand it without a thorough grounding in the classical tradition. How can anyone judge whether a new theory about the divinity of Christ (for example) has anything worthwhile to say if they do not know what the classical doctrine of the church is on the subject and how it came to be what it is? Furthermore, most of what appears as theology today will disappear in a few years – anyone who has been in the ministry for a decade or more can prove this simply by looking at the tomes which are gathering dust on his shelves, last read for some course at college and untouched since. In theology, the latest thing is also the least important, not because it has nothing to say but because what it says has not been tested by time. Even if it is very good, it will be many centuries before anyone can say whether it will last and to make it the basis for ministry today is short-sighted. A sense of perspective is desperately needed here and only a good grounding in classical theological principles can provide it.

6.6.   The way ahead

If the Anglican Communion is going to overcome its current theological crisis it must renew its foundations, which have been undermined and ignored for at least a generation. There is broad agreement about this across a wide range of churchmanship and geographical area, so in principle it ought to be fairly easy to make a case for developing theological education in ways which will inform the future clergy of our church what they are committing themselves to. Opinions may differ as to how important our heritage is for the life of the Communion today, but everyone ought to be able to agree that it should be better known than it is. For Evangelicals, the real challenge is to ensure that that heritage is fairly represented. That it might not be is clear from some of the books which have appeared in recent years. For example, a widely-used handbook of sources called *The Anglican Tradition*[131] describes the Reformation as 'the sixteenth-century emergency', which hardly captures its significance for the growth and development of Anglicanism! A more recent book of devotional pieces, called *Love's Redeeming Work*,[132] is much better at representing the Reformers, but it seriously short-changes the Evangelical tradition. One of the reasons for this is that it includes only the work of writers who have died, and since many leaders of the post-1945 Evangelical revival are happily still with us, their contribution is left out! As Evangelicals, we should not want to misrepresent others in the church or underplay the contribution they have made, and producing a book which distorts Anglicanism by slanting it too far in our direction would be counterproductive. Nevertheless, it is clear that there is a real need for material which is accessible, user-friendly and balanced in its treatment of Anglicanism, and in the current context that means putting out books which give a greater place to the Reformed and Evangelical tradition within it.

As far as dealing with heresy is concerned, it is impossible to call for theological discipline in a church which has little idea of what that might be. The key to ensuring that the Anglican Communion returns to orthodoxy can only be education. Pressure from the developing world may force the bishops at Lambeth 2008 to make a declaration in favour of the renewal of traditional Anglicanism, but it would be foolish for Anglicans in first-world countries to rely on that kind of pronouncement. After all, the 1998 Lambeth Conference made a very clear statement about the unacceptability of homosexual practice, and look what has happened since then. Grass-roots initiative is the only answer. If we as Evangelicals can co-ordinate our activities, produce the necessary materials and get to work – instead of merely organising another conference to talk about what we might do – we can make a difference in the next generation. We must be realistic about the timescale required, because we cannot put the failures of decades

---

[131] Edited by G. R. Evans and J. R. Wright (London: SPCK, 1991).
[132] Compiled by G. Rowell, K. Stevenson and R. Williams (Oxford: OUP, 2001).

right overnight. There is no 'quick fix' or short-term solution to our problems, and we must be prepared for many years of struggle, some of which will doubtless be disheartening at times. What is essential is that we should have clear aims and a workable programme to achieve them. What we want to see can be summed up as follows:

> 1. The creation of an Anglican Communion in which doctrinal orthodoxy, as defined by the Catholic creeds and the historic formularies of the Church of England, is the norm for Anglicans and not merely a tolerated option.

> 2. The creation of an expectation in the church that its accredited preachers and teachers will be well-instructed in its beliefs and committed to upholding them.

> 3. The creation of a climate of opinion which will accept that those who fail to meet these standards ought to resign their offices or failing that, be dismissed from them.

The first of these aims must be pursued throughout the Communion as a whole. We do not have to worry that the non-English churches will resent the imposition of standards originally devised for the Church of England. Most of them have grown out of that church historically and all of them have voluntarily chosen to be associated with it by being in communion with the see of Canterbury, so there should be no problem here. In fact, many of the non-English churches are fully committed to the historic formularies, and some of them have been pressing for just such a declaration from the Lambeth Conference. In insisting on this we are not trying to impose our beliefs on anyone – those who do not accept historic Anglicanism are welcome to go elsewhere and we should be prepared to regard them with as much charity as we regard members of other Christian denominations. What we are after is not exclusiveness but consistency. Just as we expect Roman Catholics to defend their beliefs and Plymouth Brethren to stand by theirs, so we should expect Anglicans to believe what the Anglican church officially professes.

In practical terms, this aim will have to be constantly restated in General Synod and in the church press so that it will be clear that it is not a passing fad espoused by a small and unrepresentative minority. There are many in the church who feel less strongly than Evangelicals do about the importance of maintaining traditional Anglican doctrine, but who also believe that honesty about what we believe is the best policy. If we can convince them to support us in this we can align ourselves with the middle ground of church opinion and shift it in our direction. There will be plenty of opposition, but we must stick to our guns and not give in to the pressure which will undoubtedly be applied. If the liberal leadership of the church realises that it has struck a rock, it will be forced to give way. There is no alternative – those who call the shots in the Anglican Communion today will not listen to the orthodox unless they have to, and we must use every legitimate means at our disposal, including the threat of withholding funds from an organisation which is not true to its principles, to get this message across.

The second aim is both easier and more difficult to achieve than the first. It is easier because it does not involve political action and the compromises which that inevitably entails, but it is also more difficult because it means persuading ordinary church members that good theology is the necessary foundation of an effective teaching and preaching ministry. To do this we shall have to produce relevant and user-friendly material for every level of church life, from the parish Bible study to the theological college lecture room. The material must not only be grounded in Scripture and faithful to its teaching, but must show how the Bible contains a consistent message (its 'systematic theology') which can be applied to real-life situations. The temptation to veer into abstraction and irrelevance, so often associated with the term 'theology', must at all costs be avoided. This is a tall order, because although there are many who profess orthodoxy there are relatively few who can apply it to the needs and conditions of modern life. We need a message which will change people's lives and lead them into a greater and growing devotion to Christ. The so-called dichotomy between the head and the heart must be overcome, and for Anglicans the obvious model for doing this must surely be the Book of Common Prayer. Where else can we find such a skillful blend of biblical content, theological construction and devotional purpose? The loss of this resource at the popular level has undone the church, which can no longer maintain the subtle but essential balance of these things which is essential to healthy spiritual growth. As a result, people have gone off in different directions and the centre has not held. We may have to update the language here and there, but that is a minor problem – what matters is that we should recover that sense of spiritual equilibrium which is the sign of a healthy Christian life and the ultimate foundation of everything we say and do as a church.

The last aim, like the first, requires constant reiteration if it is to succeed. Most of what is happening in the church today has been the work of a few people who have spent years shaping the climate of public opinion. Often they have hijacked words like 'love', 'justice' and 'integrity' so as to give the impression that those who disagree with their views are unloving, unjust and un-Christian. We do not want to imitate this tactic by defining words like 'orthodox' and 'evangelical' in ways that unchurch theologically sound people who are not conservative Evangelicals. There are many good Anglicans who do not want to be so described and who may not understand why our distinctive emphases are so important, not merely to us but to them as well. Here we must admit that we have not always put our best foot forward in the life of the wider church. It is unfortunately true that conservative Evangelicalism has often come to be associated with a superficial worship-style which ignores the great Anglican liturgical heritage and rejects anything that smacks of 'tradition'. Part of the reason for this is that many of the iconoclasts in our midst were brought up on a diet of formal religious observances which inoculated them against serious Christianity. When they later discovered a living faith, probably in a non- or para-church setting, they understandably turned against their background, which they felt had cheated them of a true experience of Christ. We must respect this feeling while at the same time recognising that forms of worship are a means to an end and not the end in themselves. It is just as wrong to insist on destroying every remnant of the past as it is to insist on maintaining all the frills of medieval pageantry. Tradition and innovation both have their place, and we should not be afraid to assert this in the face of the radical modernisers in our midst just as we have long done against the pseudo-catholic liturgical revivalists.

We must reach out to those of different churchmanships

and be fair to them, but at the same time we must protest when others label us 'fundamentalists'. In the sense that we stick to the fundamentals, the label is accurate enough, but unfortunately it has come to be associated with a kind of violent and irrational protest which is alien to our beliefs. That those who use the word intend it to be understood pejoratively can be seen from the fact that nobody ever dwells on the many virtues of 'fundamentalism'! What we want is not a slavish adherence to an orthodoxy which has been reduced to slogans and catch phrases, but a genuine commitment to the world-view which undergirds the Bible and has nurtured the Christian church from the beginning. We can no more tolerate deviation from this than the medical profession can tolerate faith healers in a hospital. There may be different opinions about how best to express our beliefs but there should be no doubt about what those beliefs are. Those who do not or who cannot accept the biblical understanding of reality have no right to be leaders and teachers in any church. Those who do not agree with the way in which that worldview has been formulated in the catholic creeds and in the Reformation formularies have no place in the Anglican Communion. There is always room for fresh thought and new ideas, but these must not contradict the faith once delivered to the saints. The wineskins may change, but the wine must retain the purity of its ancient vintage or it will taste like vinegar on the lips of the saints.

Finally, we must remember that even when we have done all we can, we are still unprofitable servants. Yet the Lord of the church has promised that if we are faithful to him, he will be faithful to us. God hears the cry of his people and demands only that we should walk in faithful obedience to him. Let us hope and pray that those who have been given the opportunity to act will accept the responsibility laid upon them and commit themselves anew to live for Christ and his glory alone. If that becomes the watchword of the Anglican Communion it will have a glorious future ahead of it and in the grace of God will be able to contribute its riches to the entire Christian world in the future as it has so often done in the past.